MY TURN

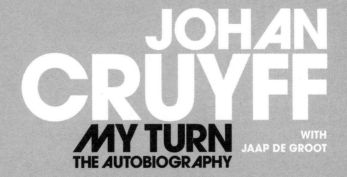

JOHAN
CRUYFF
MY TURN
THE AUTOBIOGRAPHY

WITH
JAAP DE GROOT

MACMILLAN

First published 2016 by Macmillan
an imprint of Pan Macmillan
20 New Wharf Road, London N1 9RR
Associated companies throughout the world
www.panmacmillan.com

ISBN 978-1-5098-1390-2 HB
ISBN 978-1-5098-1391-9 TPB

Visit **www.panmacmillan.com** to read more about all our books
and to buy them. You will also find features, author interviews and
news of any author events, and you can sign up for e-newsletters
so that you're always first to hear about our new releases.

Timeline

As a player

Domestic

1964 – 1973   Ajax (319 appearances, 253 goals)

1973 – 1978   Barcelona (184 appearances, 61 goals)

1979   Los Angeles Aztecs (27 appearances, 14 goals)

1980 – 1981   Washington Diplomats (32 appearances, 12 goals)

1981   Levante (10 appearances, 2 goals)

1981 – 1983   Ajax (52 appearances, 20 goals)

1983 – 1984   Feyenoord (44 appearances, 13 goals)

International

1966 – 1984   Netherlands (48 appearances, 33 goals)

Trophies

Ajax   Eredivisie 1966, 67, 68, 70, 72, 73, 82, 83;
KNVB Cup 1967, 71, 72, 83;
European Cup 1971, 72, 73;
European Super Cup 1972, 73;
Intercontinental Cup 1972

Barcelona   La Liga 1974; Copa del Rey 1978

Feyenoord   Eredivisie 1984; KNVB Cup 1984

As a manager

1985 – 1988   Ajax (KNVB Cup 1986, 87; European
Cup Winners' Cup 1987)

1988 – 1996   Barcelona (La Liga 1991, 92, 93, 94;
Copa del Rey 1992; European Cup 1992;
European Cup Winners' Cup 1989)

2009 – 2013   Catalonia

Honours

1971   Ballon d'Or

1973   Ballon d'Or

1974   Ballon d'Or and World Cup Player of the
Tournament

Significant dates

1947   (25 April) born in Amsterdam

1957   (April) joins Ajax youth team

1959   (8 July) father dies

1964   (15 November) makes first-team debut for Ajax
and scores his first goal in 3–1 defeat to GVAV

1965 – 66   scores first hat-trick and 25 goals for the
season; Ajax win Eredivisie

1966   (7 September) makes debut and scores for
Netherlands in Euro '68 qualifier against Hungary
(2–2)

1967   (6 November) becomes first Dutch international
to receive a red card

1966 – 67   is leading scorer in the league (33 goals) and Dutch Footballer of the Year; Ajax win the Eredivisie and KNVB Cup

1967 – 68   named Dutch Footballer of the Year; Ajax are Eredivisie champions for third successive year

1968   (10 December) marries Danny Coster

1969   (28 May) Ajax lose European Cup final to Milan (4–1)

1970   returns from injury wearing No. 14 shirt; he would wear the same number for the rest of his career

1970   (29 November) scores six goals in 8–1 defeat of AZ '67

1971   named Dutch and European Footballer of the Year; (2 June) Ajax win the European Cup final for the first time (2–1 vs Panathinaikos); signs seven-year deal with Ajax

1972   (31 May) scores both goals as Ajax win second European Cup (2–0 vs Inter Milan); Ajax win Intercontinental Cup

1973   (30 May) Ajax win European Cup for third successive season (1–0 vs Juventus)

1973   (19 August) plays last match for Ajax before moving to Barcelona for world record fee ($2 million approx.)

1974   (9 February) son Jordi born; birth registered in Amsterdam as name is illegal in Spain under Franco's regime

1974   (17 February) Barcelona beat Real Madrid 5–0 at the Bernabéu and go on to win La Liga for first time since 1960

1974   leads Netherlands to World Cup final, losing 2–1 to West Germany; named Player of the Tournament; first demonstrates the 'Cruyff Turn' during a group game against Sweden

1974   (December) named European Footballer of the Year

1977   (October) retires from international football

1978   (19 April) Barcelona win Copa del Rey (3–1 vs Las Palmas)

1978   Netherlands reach the World Cup final again, losing 3–1 to Argentina in extra time; Cruyff doesn't play in the tournament

1979   Barcelona's La Masia youth academy founded on Cruyff's advice

1979   moves to Los Angeles Aztecs; voted NASL Player of the Year

1980   moves to Washington Diplomats

1980   (November) rejoins Ajax, then in 8th place, as technical advisor; Ajax finish season in 2nd

1981   moves to Levante after a transfer to Leicester City falls through

1981–82   signs as a player for Ajax; Ajax win Eredivisie

1982–83   Ajax win Eredivisie and KNVB Cup double

1983–84   moves to rivals Feyenoord after Ajax fail to renew his contract; Feyenoord win the league and KNVB Cup double

1984   named Dutch Footballer of the Year for a fifth time

1984   (13 May) retires from competitive football

1985   (June) joins Ajax as technical director (de facto manager)

1985–87   Ajax win KNVB Cup in two consecutive seasons

1987   (13 May) Ajax win European Cup Winners' Cup (1–0 vs Lokomotive Leipzig)

1988   (Summer) joins Barcelona as manager

1989   (10 May) Barcelona win European Cup Winners' Cup (2–0 vs Sampdoria)

1990   (5 April) Barcelona win Copa del Rey

1991   (February) undergoes double heart bypass surgery

1992   (20 May) Barcelona win European Cup (1–0 aet vs Sampdoria)

1993   (February/March) Barcelona win European Super Cup (3–2 agg. vs Werder Bremen)

1991–94   Barcelona win La Liga four times in succession

1996   (April) is sacked as manager of Barcelona

1997   Cruyff Foundation established

1999   voted European Player of the Century and comes second to Pelé in World Player of the Century poll

1999   Cruyff Institute founded

2004	named in FIFA 100 list of the world's greatest living players
2009	100th Cruyff Court opened
2015	(October) is diagnosed with lung cancer
2016	(24 March) dies in Barcelona, aged sixty-eight

Preface

I'm not a person with college degrees. Everything I've learned, I've learned through experience. After I lost my father at the age of twelve, my life was defined by Ajax. First by my second father, who was the club's groundsman, and later by my trainers Jany van der Veen and Rinus Michels. Thanks to Ajax, I didn't just learn to be a better footballer, I learned how to behave.

Through my father-in-law I gained financial experience. When I started out, no footballer in the world had ever heard of marketing, and dealing with business was something completely new. But someone came into my life who would help me with that and bring me up. Because every time I thought I could do it on my own, things immediately went wrong. It doesn't matter. It's part of life. In the end it's more important whether you've learned from it or not.

I want to stress how important my family is. Not just my parents, my in-laws, wife, children and grandchildren, but also all the people who took me by the hand at Ajax in a phase of my life when I was very fragile. So Ajax is family to me as well. Family has also defined who I am now. Someone who has one shortcoming when it comes to football: I can only think about being at the top. As a player or a coach I'm not capable of doing something at a low level. I can only think in one direction. Upwards. To be the best possible. That's why, in the end, I had to stop. I was no longer in a physical condition to do what was needed at the top, and once that's the case you have no business being on the pitch. But because I was in a good mental state I became a coach.

Above all I want to say that my life has always been lived with a view to doing things better and getting better. I've translated that into everything I've done.

Johan Cruyff
March 2016

1

Everything I have done has been done with a view to the future, concentrating on progress, which means that the past is not something that I think about too much. For me, this is completely natural. Details of the matches I have played in have been written about better by other people elsewhere; what I am interested in is the idea of football. Continually looking forward means that I can concentrate on getting better at whatever I am doing, and I only really look back in order to gauge what I can learn from mistakes. Those lessons can be taken from different points in your life, and you don't necessarily see how connected everything is until later. So while I always move forward, I can't always look at what's gone before as a straight line. At the heart of what I have learned as a player is that, above all else, you need four things: good grass, clean changing rooms, players who clean their own boots and tight goal nets.

Everything else – skills and speed, technique and goals, will come later. This is the philosophy that defines my feeling for football and for life. I've translated that into everything I've done, whether that is with Total Football on the pitch, with my family or the Cruyff Foundation – it has always been about progress and never ever stopping getting better.

Football has been my life from the beginning. My parents owned a greengrocer's shop in Betondorp, a few hundred metres away from Ajax's De Meer Stadion in Amsterdam, so it was inevitable. My father never missed an Ajax game and, though I may not have inherited my talent from my father, he did pass on his unconditional love for the club. In fact, where my talent for football originates is a mystery. I clearly didn't learn it from my father or grandfather, as I never saw them play themselves. My uncle, Gerrit Draaijer, my mother's brother, did play a few matches at outside left for Ajax's first team, but that was in the 1950s, when Ajax were not one of Europe's well-known sides.

My father told me about players like Alfredo Di Stéfano, who understood everything about how to use space on the pitch, as well as Faas Wilkes, who was a phenomenal dribbler of the ball. He would start in midfield and dribble past four or five people. Incredible. Wilkes played for Xerxes Rotterdam, before going to Inter Milan, Torino and Valencia, returning to Holland later in his career. That was when I realized what a Dutch man could achieve on the pitch. But we didn't have a TV and didn't see many foreign teams, so for most of his career I could only watch him occasionally. As for Di Stéfano, it was not until 1962, when he came to Amsterdam with Real Madrid for the European Cup final, that I was able to see him with my own eyes.

Everything for me started in the street. The area where I lived was nicknamed the 'Concrete Village', an experiment in building cheap housing after the First World War. It was working class, and as kids we spent as much time out of the house as possible; from as early as I can remember we played football everywhere we could. It was here I learned to think about how to turn a disadvantage into an advantage. You see that the kerb isn't actually an obstacle, but that you can turn it into a teammate for a one–two. So thanks to the kerb I was able to work on my technique. When the ball bounces off different surfaces at odd angles, you have to adjust in an instant. Throughout my career people would often be surprised that I shot or passed from an angle they weren't expecting, but that's because of how I grew up. The same thing is true of balancing. When you fall on the concrete, it hurts, and, of course, you don't want to get hurt. So when playing football, you're also busy trying not to fall. It was learning to play like this, when you had to react to the situation all the time, that taught me my skills as a footballer. That's why I'm a great advocate of making young people play football without studs. They miss the hours I had in the street, the hours practising how not to fall. Give them flat soles and help them keep their balance better.

At home, life was pretty basic, but I didn't care. I grew up in a warm family home. I slept in the same room as my brother Hennie, who is two and a half years older than me. When you're very young that's a big difference. But I was out playing football as often as I could, so he had his own life and so did I.

I'm very much a mixture of my parents. I get my social side from my mother, my cunning from my father, because I'm definitely cunning. I'm always on the lookout for the best advantage, just like my father, Manus. My father was a joker. He had a glass eye and bet people five cents to see who could stare into the sun for longest. He would put his hand on his good eye, look at the sun for a minute and pick up his money. My mother, Nel, was very sociable. For her, everything revolved around the family. She had nine brothers and sisters, so in addition to nine uncles and aunts, I also had dozens of cousins. The great thing was that if anything bad happened there was always someone who could help you. One of them knew about heating stoves, another was good at drawing, so there was always someone whose door you could knock on if there was a problem. But when it came to football, I was on my own – the interest in it I had seemed to have passed them all by.

I went to the Groen van Prinsterer School in Amsterdam, which was a Christian school, even though I wasn't brought up in the faith and there were also secular schools nearby. I only ever went into a church to deliver an order for my father, and when I asked my father why I had to go to the school with the Bible in my bag, he said: 'Johan, they tell good stories there. I'm trying to give you as much as possible in that way, and later you can decide for yourself about what to do with it.'

Even at school I wanted to play football, and from a very young age I was soon well known as the boy with the ball. Every day I took my ball into class with me, placed it under my desk and passed it between my feet throughout the lesson. Sometimes the teacher sent me outside because I was too much of a nuisance. I was doing it so instinctively that I wasn't even aware that I was busy kicking the ball from left foot to right. Apart from that, I didn't really get much out of my time at school, although what I do remember above all from my schooldays is that I never bunked off. Even though I wasn't wild about learning, I understood it was something I had to do, and I stuck with it until I was old enough to decide for myself that I didn't want that any more.

In contrast, I remember the first time I went to Ajax as

if it was yesterday. It was 1952, I think, so I was about five. My father asked if I wanted to go with him to deliver baskets of fruit for the players who were sick or injured, so I rode my bike with him down the road to the club, so excited to be able to walk through its doors for the first time, and not just sit in the stands. It was then that I met Henk Angel, a friend of my father who was working as a groundsman there. Henk asked me if I wanted to give him a hand, and I started the very next day. So, at the age of five, my life with Ajax began. I think back on my childhood with great fondness. I've known nothing but love. At home, but also at Ajax. It was thanks to Uncle Henk, who let me do all kinds of odd jobs in the stadium when the pitches had just been laid or were unplayable in winter, that I spent so much time at the club. As a reward, I was allowed to play football in the hall or in the main stands. I also spent time during the summer holidays at the home of Arend van der Wel, an Ajax forward who had become a family friend. He had just moved from Ajax to Sportclub Enschede, and had a nice life in the countryside. It was there that I had my first driving lessons, aged seven or eight, sitting on Arend's lap behind the wheel. It was also at Sportclub Enschede that I met Abe Lenstra, the brilliant forward who had just moved there from Heerenveen. He was a complete icon in those days. I even kicked a ball about with him once at training, and that was something special. But what I mostly remember about Abe is that he always had a ball with him.

During my early years I saw a lot of Uncle Henk, particularly after his wife passed away, as he often ate at our house. Over meals I listened breathlessly to what was happening at Ajax. It was during this time, when I was a young boy, that Arend van der Wel also joined us for meals. Back then he was still a young player with the first eleven and lived in Amsterdam North, which was too far to go home after work and get back in time for evening training, so he ate with us. Thus, from a very early age, I not only was spending all my free time at the Ajax stadium, but also had the club as a presence in our house, and it was thanks to Uncle Henk, as we continued to call him even after my father died and he married my mother, and Arend, that from the age of five I learned everything that was going on at the club from the changing room to the first eleven. I sat listening to them day after day, soaking it all up like a sponge.

As soon as I was old enough I was running about all over the place on my own, playing football in the streets with my friends, and from then on the Ajax stadium became my second home. I was there every spare moment, and never left home without a football. From the age of five, when I went to help out with Uncle Henk at the stadium, I always took my bootbag with me as well. You never knew if the team might be a man short for training or a practice match and I was often lucky, though usually only because they felt sorry for me. I was a bag of bones, I looked like a shrimp, and they took pity on me, which meant that even though I had no business being there, and wasn't even in the youth team, I was playing with the Ajax team from a very early age. It was another example of a belief that I have always had and tried to pass on – that you can turn a disadvantage, like my scrawny appearance, into an advantage.

I am often asked what my greatest memory was as a footballer. Honestly, I cannot remember much of the details, even things like my first goal at home for Ajax after turning pro. What I do remember, though, and very clearly, was the first time I was allowed on the pitch in a full stadium. Not as a footballer, but to aerate the goal area with a pitchfork. I was about eight years old, my father was still alive, and I wasn't even on the books, but here I was out on the pitch, in front of a full stadium, helping to make it perfect for the first team. That's not the kind of thing you ever forget. As I jabbed the fork into the turf, I felt responsible for delivering the perfect playing surface for my heroes. As someone who has played and managed and watched and thought about football all my life, I am sure that such early experiences of helping to take care of things, learning the importance of those kinds of standards, informed the person I became. After I retired from playing and managing and set up the Cruyff Foundation to help give kids a chance to play football, we drew up a list of fourteen rules that people had to respect. Number two on the list was about responsibility and respect for the pitch and the people, and that all stemmed from this time in my life. As I have said, all my life lessons were learned while at Ajax.

Even though I was a mediocre student, from an early age I had an affinity with numbers. Numerology interests me. So, for example, I married Danny on the second day of the twelfth month, December. Two plus twelve produces the number on my back: number fourteen. The year was 1968, and six plus eight is also fourteen. No wonder we're still together after forty-eight years. Our marriage was good twice over. The same is true of my son, Jordi. He was born in '74 and I was born in '47. So both years add up to eleven. And his birthday is on 9 February and mine's 25 April. That's nine plus two and two plus five plus four. Both eleven.

I'm even good at remembering phone numbers. My friends just have to give me their number once and I'll never forget it. Maybe that's why I'm also good at mental arithmetic. I didn't learn it at school, but in my parents' greengrocery. When my father was off doing deliveries and my mother had to cook our meals, it was my job to help the customers. But I was still too small to reach the till. So I learned mental arithmetic, and because I was good at it from a very young age I think that's where my fascination began. I also think it was, in part, because of this love of numbers, learning about the mental side of things, that I started thinking more about numbers in football – how we can take advantage of the opposition, how we can work better with the space, like Di Stéfano had done. So, while my parents didn't give me footballing skill, they did give me a way of thinking about football that was different.

In terms of the fitness that was required as a footballer, I've always had a terrible aversion to cross-country running, and the medicine balls that we had to use in the gym. When I was in the Ajax first team, every time Rinus Michels sent us off into the forest I tried to get as far ahead as possible, then hide behind a tree until the team returned, hoping no one would do a head count on the route. That worked for a while, until Michels worked out what was going on. As punishment I had to do a disciplinary training session at the forest track at eight in the morning on my day off. Michels drove up exactly on time. He was in his pyjamas behind the wheel, he wound down the window and said, 'It's far too cold for me, I'm going back to bed.' Leaving me humiliated.

I officially joined the Ajax youth system in 1957, at the age of ten. I was a scrawny kid when I joined, and if I had signed up now I am sure that they would have put me through all sorts of exercise routines. But I had none of that, and would have hated it. The most that I did was ask my mother to cook me more green beans and spinach, because of the iron. As for the rest, I just did what I had always done, which was spend all my free time playing football, either at the club or on the street with my friends. What has been important to me is not only playing football, but enjoying it.

Later, I had something similar when I coached Frank Rijkaard at Ajax, who always pretended he needed to cough during cross-country circuit training. The players were usually split into two groups, one following the other. He would join the second group, let his teammates run on and then join the forward group on their next circuit. That way he ensured that he ended up running one lap less than the rest. No other trainer noticed, but I did. I just enjoyed it. Of course, I told him later on, but at the same time I had a really good laugh about it. I love that kind of cunning, thanks to my father, although I actually had a lot of my mother in me too. Later, when I started going out with Danny, I sometimes wanted to stay out longer than Michels allowed. He always drove through Amsterdam in the evening to check if our cars were parked outside the house on time. Once I borrowed my stepfather's car and left my own car at home. Michels suspected what I'd done and threatened to give me a fine the next day. I was still living at home, and I said, 'Just call my mother, I was at home.' He did, and she played along perfectly, Michels had to withdraw the threat and I had a great laugh with my mother later on.

When I was with the Ajax youth team at the age of twelve, Jany van der Veen trained me not only in football, but also in norms and values. He was the first person at

Ajax who taught me always to choose a particular course and follow it. He was another example of how the Ajax life was one that compensated for the education that I wouldn't be getting at school. Jany only ever worked with the youth team, but he took the ideas he had worked on with Jack Reynolds – the visionary Englishman who had been the first team coach in the 1940s and helped lay the footballing foundations that Total Football would later be built on – and applied them to us. It was Jany who taught us to play games in which we would work on mistakes so that we could be creative in the way we practised. From Michels we got the discipline, but it was from Jany that we got the fun. When I became a coach myself, I took these ideas to Barcelona. As I always said, if you work in football, it's not work. You have to train hard, but you have to have fun as well.

My trainers while I was in the youth squad were Vic Buckingham, who was manager of the first team before Michels, Keith Spurgeon, who would also manage the first team for a season, and, most importantly, Jany van der Veen, the youth team coach. Van der Veen always insisted on very specific training, in which five fundamentals played a central part. Playing games always alternated with maintaining and developing these five basic fundamentals of football: shooting, heading, dribbling, passing and controlling the ball. So we were always really busy with the ball. This way of training has always remained the standard for me. It's led me to realize that the easiest way is often the hardest. So I see touching the ball once as the highest form of technique. But to be able to touch the ball perfectly once, you need to have touched it a hundred thousand times in training, and that's what we spent our time doing. This was

the school of thought at Ajax, which would go on to produce players who were technically up there with the best
in the world. All thanks to the apparently simple training
techniques of people like van der Veen.

But he wasn't the only one. I owe something else to Vic
Buckingham, who later started me off in the first team
when I was seventeen. He had two sons my age, who were
still finding their way around Amsterdam, and because my
mother cleaned for the Buckingham family I often went to
their house, which is how I learned English. Not at school,
but by talking to the Buckingham family a lot. This was the
Ajax way of doing things – to look after the young kids in
the team and make sure they behaved properly. And of the
footballers, when I started to play for the first team, Piet
Keizer took me under his wing. He was almost four years
older than me and had been playing in the first team for
three seasons by the time I was picked. Ajax were only just
starting to offer professional contracts, and Piet was the
first to receive one. I was the second, and I noticed that Piet
was fond of me. For example, he always made sure that I
was home by half past nine in the evening, so that I would
avoid a fine or punishment from Michels.

While it was Buckingham who gave me a place in the
first team, it was Michels – who took over in 1965 – with
who I had the most special bond. It was Michels who
shielded the team from the rest of the club's management
structure, which was completely amateur. When Michels
arrived, we were near the bottom of the league, and he tried
to protect us from what was happening off the pitch to
make sure that everything we did was focused on getting us
to play better and think more clearly about the game. It was
him who managed Ajax to the very top of the game. The

bond that we created at Ajax was the sort of thing that is difficult to put into words, because he became part of my life outside the club. Much later on, when I had kids of my own, he dressed up as Santa Claus at a children's party at our house. But my daughter Chantal recognized him. I can still hear her saying, 'Hey, you're not Santa at all, you're Uncle Rinus.'

I was eighteen years old when Michels took over, the youngest player in the team, but he would take me aside and talk about the tactics of the game. He didn't do this with anyone else, and it was through those conversations that we formed a bond. We talked about how we could get better if we did certain things, and, I realize now, it was in these conversations that we developed the ideas that would shape the unique way Ajax came to play in the late 1960s, while every other club was doing the things they had always done. He would explain to me how he wanted to play and what needed to be done if something went wrong. Henk Angel, Arend van der Wel, Jany van der Veen, Rinus Michels, Piet Keizer and many others helped to define what I became in the end. At important moments in my life they also went out of their way for me off the field as well. But it was Michels who drove me to the doctor because, after my father passed away, we didn't have a car at home any more. Less agreeable things happened between Michels and me later on, but they never tainted the image I had of the man who stood up for me when, as a young guy, I really needed him.

My father died in 1959, when he was forty-five and I was twelve. It was the day I got my lower school certificate and

I heard that he was dead during the farewell party. After that, Ajax started to play an even bigger part in my life, because I no longer had my father at home to turn to. We found out that he had died of a heart attack because his cholesterol was too high. His death has never let go of me, and as I grew older, the feeling that his fate would also be mine grew stronger. For a long time, I thought that I wouldn't make fifty. So I wasn't really very surprised when I developed heart problems at about the same age as my father, while I was coaching at Barcelona, because I had more or less prepared myself for it. Except for one big difference – thirty years later medical science was able to save me.

My father is, like my mother, buried in Amsterdam's eastern cemetery, which is right by the old Ajax stadium, and not long after he was buried I started talking to him whenever I walked, cycled or drove past the graveyard. I did this for a long while after he died. To start with I talked to him about school, then later, when I was playing for Ajax, I talked to him mostly about football: what a dick the referee was, how I'd scored my goals, that kind of thing. Over the years our conversations changed but never ceased. I always went to talk to him to ask his advice every time I had to make a difficult decision in my life. 'So, what do you think, Dad?' Then I got up next morning and knew what I needed to do. I still have no idea how it worked, but he was there every time I had to make a decision, and after I had talked to him I knew exactly the right thing to do.

One time, I would have been in my early twenties by this point, I was still living in Amsterdam, had just got married and was playing regularly for the first team. Things were good, but there were a lot of rows at Ajax at the time, and I was racked with doubts about certain things, even about the help my father still seemed to be giving me. I am not very religious, and I started wondering how this was happening. After all, nobody's ever come back from the dead. That's when I put my father on the spot a bit. I asked him to stop my watch whenever he was nearby, in whatever form, to show that he was really there and could hear what I was saying. It may be coincidence, but the next morning my watch had stopped. My father-in-law owned a watch shop, and a watchmaker there looked at it the same day, couldn't find anything wrong and soon got it going again. The very next morning it was the same story – my watch had stopped again. Once more I went back to the shop, and again they couldn't find anything amiss. That evening I told my father he'd convinced me that he had heard everything I had said, and the next day my watch was still going and has never stopped since. I wear it every day.

In the months after my father's death my mother had to earn some money, and because of the close connection with the club through my father and Uncle Henk, as well as because I was hanging around all the time, Ajax looked after our family. One thing they did was find her the work as a house cleaner for the English trainers that Ajax had at the time, which led to me getting to know the Buckingham family. The club also employed her to clean the changing rooms. A few years later, when my mother married Uncle Henk, who became a second father to me and still worked at the club, my connection to Ajax was complete.

Even though my mother was now earning money, there wasn't enough spare to pay for us to go on holiday now, so I spent the whole year at De Meer, even after the season had finished. Whatever the month, I was always there playing football. In the summer, when the football season had finished, baseball was played at Ajax, and I was very good at that, too. As a catcher I was even on the Dutch national team until I was fifteen. I was also the first hitter, but I was so small that they could never pitch three strikes. So it was often four wide and straight for home base.

Baseball allowed me to focus on a lot of details that would later be very useful to me in football. As a catcher you determine the pitcher's throw because he doesn't have an overview of the whole field and you do. I learned that you had to know where you were going to throw the ball before you received it, which meant that you had to have an idea of all the space around you and where each player was before you made your throw. No football coach ever told me that I had to know where I was going to pass the ball before I had received it, but later on when I was playing football professionally the lessons from baseball – to focus on having a total overview – came back to me, and became my strength. Baseball is typically one of those sports that can bring on a talent during training, because there are lots of parallels with football. Like starting speed, sliding, spatial insight, learning to think a move ahead and much more besides. These are the same sort of principles that Barcelona have with their close control and passing drills like the rondo, which are the foundation of their tiki-taka style.

I know for certain that it worked for me because I continued to immerse myself in baseball later on, which meant that as a coach I was able to transfer a lot of advice from baseball to football very successfully. The same was true of learning to think ahead, which was what baseball taught me as well. You're always busy making decisions between space and risk in fractions of a second. To be good at baseball required you to bridge the gap between runner and home, and get the ball there before the runner arrives. It also taught me about tactical insight – making the right decision and performing it in a technically good way. It was only later that I pulled this together to create my vision of how the game of football should be played. I absorbed all these lessons without noticing the bigger picture at the time. I was just a kid who had a ball every waking minute of every day.

My period with the Ajax youth team – between ten and seventeen – was a beautiful time, because there was nothing at stake. Everyone was helping me get better, and I was still to achieve something. It was only later on when I started talking about tactics – first as a player, then as a coach – that I realized the importance of what I had been exposed to and made the connection between what was going on in front of me, say in a game against Real Madrid, and what I had experienced as a kid. And because I had subconsciously absorbed everything – always watching, listening – I developed really quickly as a footballer. It also helped that for a long time I played for two different teams. Even after I'd made my first-team debut as an outfield player with Ajax when I was seventeen, on 15 November 1964, I continued to play in goal for the third team. I enjoyed that enormously. I was also really good at it and one year I was even reserve goalie when Ajax played in the European Cup, because in those days only one substitute was allowed on the bench.

Michels and Jany also taught us that we had to become psychologically strong. I still remember the mental trick Jany first used on me when I was still only fifteen or sixteen, but which continued when I was playing in the first team under Vic Buckingham, and later with Rinus Michels. Van der Veen saw to it that I first had to play one half with the juniors and then the next day I was a substitute with the first team, and was sometimes given some playing time. This made me feel that, because I'd been playing for the first team, I was morally obliged to be the best player in the juniors. This is how I thought the game should be played, and every match was about trying to get closer to being the best, whichever team I was playing for. People said that I talked too much, and people got annoyed with me for doing so, telling me to shut up the whole time. I was at the stadium all day every day, so when I got a chance to play, it wasn't strange to me because I had known these players for over half my life. I was a kid having fun, and for the first fifteen years of my life there was no philosophy and no analysis. It was just fun. I had no feeling of failure. I just took everything as it came and loved it.

In 1965, a few months after my debut, Ajax offered me my first contract. As I said, I was only the second player to sign full-time with Ajax after Piet – the rest of the squad were still part-time – but I was still doing odd jobs, living my life. I spent most of the time on the street with the ball and it was only when I met Danny that I got a bank account and started to plan. I signed the contract in the presence of my mother and when we left the office I immediately told her that she'd cleaned the changing rooms for the last time the day before. I didn't want her to have to go to work in the room that I'd just dirtied. She still washed my football kit at home for a while because we didn't have the money for a washing machine, and I had to save up for a few months to buy one.

These days it might be difficult to grasp that a so-called 'star player' would have to take his dirty kit home to be washed, but experience like that does shape you. It shapes you in terms of looking after your clothes, it shapes you in terms of cleaning your boots and it shapes you as a person. Later, as a trainer, I tried to communicate that to the youth players. With the veiled message that, if you clean your own boots, you know what kind of studs you have under them and you end up with a better feeling for your environment. As a trainer, you also hope to give your players a good social grounding. If that didn't work, when I was coach at Ajax and then at Barcelona I'd have two or three players clean the changing room to strengthen their sense of responsibility. Such behaviour, I have discovered, is important in football because you're putting into practice outside the game something that you have learned within it. But this discovery came much later. Although I have made a virtue of it, the simple fact that I had to wash my dirty kit at home, of course, says a lot about how unprofessionally Ajax was organized around 1965, my second year in the first team.

Because Piet Keizer and I were the only full-time professional players, we could only train with the full team in the evenings because everyone else had jobs, like running a tobacconist's shop. During the day there were usually about seven of us at the stadium altogether, and in the evening the others could pop out to train for a few hours if they felt like it. But that situation didn't last long. Especially when, after Vic Buckingham's second spell as manager ended in January 1965, Rinus Michels took over.

2

In the end, the period of professional growth for the club lasted nine years, running from the start of my first full season in the Eredivisie in 1965 until the World Cup Final in Munich in 1974. In less than ten years we took Ajax from the unknown to the Total Football that the world still talks about. A question often asked is whether this kind of revolution is still possible. I think it is, in fact I'm pretty sure. The proof was delivered by Ajax in the 1980s and 1990s, and then also more recently by Barcelona and Bayern Munich.

The basis of Ajax's big breakthrough was a combination of talent, technique and discipline. As I've said, Jany van der Veen and Rinus Michels played a big part in that. Van der Veen not only taught us a love of football and the club, but was able to work on our technique in a very refined way. He also had an eye for tricks on the field that we absorbed into our positional play. What I learned was that football is a process of making mistakes, then analysing them to learn lessons and not get frustrated. We were getting better each year, and I never looked back. At the end of each game I was already thinking about the next and what I could do better. Following on from van der Veen's training, we further developed our footballing skills with Michels. This kind of professionalization of the team meant that we could train as a unit during the day, and become much better, both technically and physically, as a result. Once that had been achieved, he hammered away at our mentality. The special thing was that following his instructions never created an atmosphere of rigid obedience.

Within Ajax there was always space for self-mockery and humour. I think this combination was vitally important in developing the aura that we built around us as a team. We knew what we were doing, and we did it with pleasure. That was often the most intimidating thing for our opponents. And because that was the atmosphere that I was surrounded by at the club from a very young age, I never felt scared of failure or worried about an upcoming match. Because I'd been at the De Meer almost every day from the age of five, I knew all the first-eleven players when I was put into the first team, which meant that the step-up from the juniors wasn't in any way daunting for me. That was how I approached every game. The only thing that I was interested in, other than playing the game, was explaining the tactics we used. Before I got married I didn't think about the future, I was living my life one day at a time, enjoying myself. I wasn't interested in the step beyond. I was mad about football and thought playing matches was great, and it didn't matter to me whether it was in the juniors, the third team or the first.

That didn't change much even later on, when I played in the big matches, including my debut with the Dutch national team in 1966, and later my first European Cup game. I went out there and played as I always had done. In those days Michels called me a rough diamond, but he always made sure I was involved, such as when he held those separate pre-match discussions about our opponents and our tactics with me. In that way he taught me at a young age to think about team play. I later adapted that same method with players like Marco van Basten and Pep Guardiola. It works in two directions: it's good for the team and it's good for the player in question.

Of course, you make mistakes as a young player. But that's part of the learning process you're in the middle of. Like the first time I was sent off the field. It was during my second international with the Dutch national team, against Czechoslovakia in 1967. I was constantly being kicked from the first whistle, but the referee, Rudi Glöckner from East Germany, did nothing about it. Eventually I asked him why he was always letting the defenders get away with it, but he just told me to keep my mouth shut. When I received an almighty great kick right under his nose a little later and he didn't blow his whistle, I brought the subject up again. I was sent off, and I was banned from playing for the national team for a year. It turned into a huge row, and it was probably the first time the discussion about a footballer's right to protest was set in motion, but I knew I was completely within my rights. The Czechs were busy kicking me out of the match, the referee just let it happen, and in the end he attacked me because I was asking why he wasn't doing anything. Nowadays, the players and the referee are jointly responsible for ensuring that the public are kept as entertained as possible, but in 1967 that still was absolutely not the case. The ref was the boss and no one questioned his authority, and that is without mentioning the huge social difference between me, a young Western sportsman in the age of Beatlemania, and an East German who had to rule the field once a week for ninety minutes and then go back to keeping his trap shut in the GDR.

At Ajax, where I was allowed to carry on playing despite

the national team ban, there were advantages and disadvantages that we also had to deal with. After we'd been crowned champions in my first season, 1965–66, we were due to play Liverpool in the second round of the 1966–67 European Cup. At that time, Liverpool were not just the best club in England, but one of the strongest teams in the world. Although as a general rule I'm bad at remembering games and matches and events, I can still remember pretty much everything about the legendary *mistwedstrijd* ('fog game') in the Olympic Stadium in Amsterdam and the return match at Anfield in Liverpool. Remember that England had just won the World Cup, so everyone was talking about them, and the Liverpool team included players like Ron Yeats, Ian St John, Tommy Lawrence and Peter Thompson, good footballers that we had all heard about. Everyone said that we were going to lose, but at half time we went in 4–0 up. The game had nearly been postponed because of heavy fog – no one was happy with the visibility but both teams had to play in the conditions. But the main reason I remember the tie so clearly is because in those games against Liverpool we had confirmation that we were technically superior, and that everything Michels was putting in place was working. In a technical sense, the English champions were blown away. In Amsterdam the final score was 5–1 and I still remember their manager Bill Shankly saying after the end of the game that it was a freak result and it would be 7–0 in Liverpool.

A week later we achieved another kind of breakthrough. I stood on the pitch at Anfield with goosebumps. Not because I was scared of our opponents, but because of the atmosphere. The huge Kop stand where the most fanatical supporters were, and all their singing: Anfield was incredibly impressive. I really enjoyed it for ninety minutes, and we played a magnificent game. Even though it was a 2–2 draw, we were in complete control. My happiness at our progress and at getting into the next round was matched only by the impression Anfield left on me; from that evening English football had captured my heart. I had only played football at the highest level for a few seasons and I had never seen anything like this – the passion for the game, and how much the fans wanted their team to win, and it made me think that one day I would like to play in England. Unfortunately, that dream didn't come to pass, because in those days borders were still closed to foreign players. Even today I still think that was a terrible shame.

After the elimination of Liverpool everyone was saying that we had a chance of winning the European Cup, but in the quarter-final we were eliminated by Dukla Prague 3–2 on aggregate. Unjustly and unfortunately, to a late own goal, but it did happen. And of course I learned from it again, because this was the philosophy that shaped the way we thought and talked about football. Every game we were getting better, and every game we were taking a step in the direction that Michels wanted us to go. We wanted to win games, but we also wanted to entertain the fans and send them home happy. That's not an easy thing to do, but the victory over Liverpool showed that by now Ajax were taking steps in the right direction. The Liverpool game was so important to us because of Shankly's jibe that he had never heard of Ajax (although that wasn't as bad as Max Merkel of FC Nürnberg, who said he thought we were a cleaning product). But until the Liverpool game we meant very little to anyone internationally. After that game it all changed.

The following year we were unlucky enough to draw Real Madrid, the great team of that time, in the first round, but we moved another step closer to greatness by taking the tie to extra time and only suffering a narrow defeat. The year after that, in 1969, we made a further advance by reaching the European Cup final, losing against AC Milan 4–1. That was when Michels brought in six or seven new players. Vasović was brought in to play *libero* or sweeper – the last man in defence, and he was good for security at the back. Later, Horst Blankenburg took over from Vasović because he was more of an attacking player, he was more skilful, whereas Vasović brought more power to the team. You wouldn't dare mess around with Vasović. As a striker you knew you were in trouble with him. Most importantly, he was physically strong, as well as strong mentally, and he had played European football. The switch was one step closer to Total Football.

Then, in 1971, we won the European Cup for the first time, and won it the next two years as well. So, within six years Ajax had gone from being an average club to the best team in the world. And what was the secret? It was simple – it was a combination of talent, technique and discipline, which were all things that we had been working on at Ajax, even before Michels had arrived. It was what it meant to be part of the club. What Michels brought, and he and I talked about all the time, was the importance of organization on the field. It was here that my love of mental arithmetic came to the fore, in understanding how we could make the most of the pitch in front of us to beat the opposition. Once you understand completely how to organize a team, then you know what the possibilities are. This is what we achieved at Ajax before any other team.

For example, at Ajax we had what we called the tutti-frutti side on the left and the serious side on the right. On the right, with Wim Suurbier, Johan Neeskens and Sjaak Swart, you had sound security; on the left you never knew what was going to happen with Ruud Krol, Gerrie Mühren, Piet Keizer and yours truly. So we had a perfect mixture of technique, tactics, performance and footballing style, which would win games, but just as importantly it made the crowds happy – I understood that that was a vital part of my job as well. The spectators had been working all week; we had to entertain them on their day off with fine football, and at the same time get a good result.

The good player is the player who touches the ball just once and knows where to run; that is what Dutch football is about. I have always said that football should be played beautifully, and in an attacking way. It must be a spectacle. At Ajax, what we loved were technique and tactics. Every trainer talks about movement, about running a lot and putting a shift in. I say don't run so much. Football is a game you play with your brains. You have to be in the right place at the right moment, not too early, not too late.

Looking back, it all came together in that game against Brazil in the 1974 World Cup, when Michels had taken over the national team. Until then, no one really knew how good we were, and the game against Brazil was probably the moment you could point to and say *that* was Total Football. When we walked onto the pitch we were nervous, because we thought that we were still playing the team of 1970, which had won the World Cup. It took us thirty minutes to realize that we were actually more skilful than them. We were still discovering our own skills, and then we realized that we could actually win. Winning was the consequence of the process that we had concentrated on. The first step was to bring enjoyment to the crowd, the next was the win. I had no real idea of the significance of it all at the time, and it was only when I became ill that I got an idea of how important what we did as a team was. It was pretty special, what we achieved.

In that period from 1968 onwards what I learned from Michels left an indelible mark on how I understood the game. Like his belief that defence is a matter of giving your opponent as little time as possible, or that when you've got possession of the ball you have to ensure that you have as much space as possible, and when you lose the ball you must minimize the space your opponent has. In fact, everything in football is a function of distance. Then there are the ten thousand hours of training spent on the practical side of things. On the pitch I was looking at all the options, but I only looked at it from my own perspective. I was interested in the process. If you were able to analyse your next step then you had a chance of making the next step successfully. When I look back, I can see that we were making progress. I don't think I was taught much, but the biggest lessons were from falling and failing. What had happened had happened, and I tried to learn something new from it and move on to the next chapter. I have never looked back much, and when I closed the door at home, even when we had lost, I was able to put it all behind me and forget about it. That's why I was never good at remembering details of games, or even the goals that I had scored. I was always much more interested in the process. The way I analysed was through a sixth sense. I didn't need to go back and look at games to know what we needed to do.

By the end of my time at Ajax I'd won the European Cup three times, and been named European player of the year in 1971 and 1972, which was nice but, really, what are trophies and medals other than mementoes of the past? At home I have nothing on my walls about football. When I was awarded an honour, the medal I was given disappeared into my grandchildren's toy box. Football is a game of mistakes. What I loved was the mathematics of the game, the analysis, how to improve. People often ask how we did it, what happened in the dressing room, and how we created Total Football, but for me this is not what was important. We had an instinct, we had been playing together for years, and knew each other very well, that was the most important thing. Of course, money is a factor – although, as I have said before, I've never seen a bag of money score a goal – but the fundamental idea is teamwork: arrive as a team, leave as a team and return home as a team.

We enjoyed some good results in those years at Ajax, and played some good football too, but I hope that I will be remembered not just as a football player, but as someone who was trying to improve all the time. For example, the European Cup we won at Wembley in 1971 against Panathinaikos was not a good game because many of the players had problems with pressure. The final in 1972, against Inter Milan, was a much better expression of Total Football.

A lot of people remember my goal against Ado den Haag in 1969, the so called 'curve goal'. For me it was pure intuition, but it gives me a good feeling that people are still talking about it. It was good technique, yes, but I had no other options. Still, it made people happy, and we won the game. It was only later on that I realized how important it was and the impact. I controlled a long clearance from our defence with my right foot on the left-hand side of the pitch – I was busy tying up my sock when the ball was passed from deep so I was still clutching the piece of string that held up my socks in my hand – and because the ball was still spinning when I hit it towards the goal it curved in over the keeper. Like I said, it was pure intuition. Like any trick I ever did, I hadn't practised it – the idea just came to me. It was only later that it came to have meaning.

During the first part of my life I followed no philosophy, I absorbed as much as I could, I lived day to day. I did have experiences that gave me insight later on, when the seeds were sown ready for harvest time. It was only later that I realized that the foundations of everything I created were laid down at that earlier time. If my development as a footballer was perfectly normal, things happening outside weren't. I took my mother to my first contract negotiation, and once that was over I seemed to trip over everything. Particularly when it came to the media and commerce, because suddenly things were moving very quickly. I even made a record, and my marriage to Danny appeared on the front pages. I often liked the publicity, but sometimes it was too much. I joined in with everything, while in reality I hadn't a clue about anything. That was why the arrival of Cor Coster in my life was a gift from God. Danny's father was a diamond dealer in Amsterdam and a hard-headed businessman. The first time I visited my in-laws, he asked me if I had a savings account. I hadn't, I told him. In fact, the only thing I understood was football. Cor was bewildered, and started looking after my affairs.

From that moment I said to Ajax: 'Just talk to him, he's come to help me.' At first they didn't want to do that, and in 1968, three years after I had signed my first contract, I brought him along for the first time to negotiate on my behalf. For a player to have any sort of representation was unheard of at the time, and the board were thunderstruck, insisting that he had no business being there. So I said: 'But there are six of you sitting here, why can't I have somebody on my side?' When they stood their ground, we walked out. Later, they allowed Cor to negotiate on my behalf. The club weren't happy about it, but in the end Cor helped a lot, and not just me, but all Dutch footballers, assisting with the set-up of a pension scheme at a time when there were absolutely no financial arrangements in place to support players once their careers were over.

The collaboration between Cor and myself soon became a full-time job for him. No one could get round Cor, and he was always keeping me out of trouble. That was why his death in 2008 had such a huge impact on me. He has been enormously important in my life, and not just for me as a footballer, but also as a father figure, father-in-law, the grandfather of our children, and simply as a human being.

Cor also guided me socially. The most important thing he taught me was to have self-respect, and he understood that his role was to nurture me in a particular way. As a well-known footballer you were actually walking into an unreal world, everything is abnormal – the salary, the media interest – and at a time like that your business manager must ensure his talent isn't going off in twelve directions at the same time. The risk for footballers has only grown over the years. Not least because of social media. A lot of footballers make a point of saying that they have a lot of followers, but whom do they follow? Nobody, as far as I can see. That's not being tough, it's a limitation. Cor understood that better than anybody; he ensured that I developed well not only as a footballer, but also as a person who had to get on with his life once the football was over. Unfortunately, there are so few players' agents these days who understand this that I often wonder whose interests they actually serve. The interests of the footballer or their own businesses? I'd even go one step further. When an agent is really committed to football, he should keep an eye on the interests not just of his player, but also of his club. Which means working out what a club can and cannot afford to do, just as my father-in-law did during the negotiations with Ajax and, later, Feyenoord.

In my view money is very important in football, but it should always come second to the game. If money comes first, you're doing things the wrong way round. Where that's concerned I cite the great teams from history: Ajax, Real Madrid, Barcelona, Bayern Munich, AC Milan and Manchester United. All their teams had a solid core that derived from their own youth teams, and players who have the club's DNA inside them always bring something extra as well. That's why I don't understand why the English Premier League does so little about player development. Is the level of play really improved that much by spending all those billions? Not at all. I know for sure that the process we started with Ajax in 1965 is still working today. Good training and strong leadership, along with a combination of talent, technique and discipline.

*

In 1973, Ajax were unbeatable. For three years we had won everything there was to win. For the last two seasons that happened without Rinus Michels, who moved to FC Barcelona after the first European Cup win in 1971. He was succeeded at Ajax by the Romanian Ştefan Kovács. A nice guy, but a lot less disciplined. And if you have less discipline coming from the coach, you end up with lots of different opinions coming from the squad. Kovács was the kind of trainer who said, 'Right, guys, these are the rules. Think about it, do this, do that and develop yourselves.' Things went well at first. Despite the inevitable differences of opinion in the changing room as the players developed themselves individually, our group discipline still held together. After we won our second European Cup, in 1972, however, the cracks began to show. The final against Inter Milan was the best of our three by some distance. We won 2–0, having kept up the pressure on the Italians from the first minute to the last. I had a good game, scoring both goals. The whole world raved about the match. It was football at its finest, once again in a final. But within the club people had started getting ideas above their station. It started with Kovács's vision: he encouraged self-development among his players, but he didn't apply the same principle to himself.

Allowing players free rein creates difficulties in relationships inside the team. If everyone had had his own opinions, but had put the collective good of the team first, it wouldn't have mattered so much. But that wasn't what happened. Not only that, but some players either felt alienated because they didn't understand what they were being asked to do, or refused to accept the fact that what they were doing wouldn't achieve the desired result.

That was why I left Ajax for Barcelona in August 1973. The move was unexpected, not least by me. The club had just won its third consecutive European Cup, I'd not long ago extended my contract for another seven years, I'd just become a father and I'd decided to bring my children up in the Netherlands because it was a familiar environment. I thought I had secured my future and that of my family in every respect. Soon I learned that I'd done no such thing. Under Kovács, I felt the situation at Ajax was rapidly going from bad to worse, so much so that I couldn't stay there. While Michels had always planned our training sessions, Kovács style of self-development was undermining discipline both in training and on match days.

Because I was arguably the best footballer at the club, and certainly the most famous, Kovács's methods tended to make me the centre of attention. But people often forget that my teammates were exceptionally good footballers too, and certainly better in their individual roles – full back, midfield, outside left or whatever – than I could ever be. So why should I always be in the spotlight? Unfortunately, it must have seemed to many of the team that I was just attention seeking.

The last straw was the vote on the captaincy. It happened in the training camp, just before the start of the 1973–74 season. Kovács had left the club during the summer and been replaced by George Knobel, but the damage had already been done. I thought it was weird that we even needed to have a vote. I'd just suggested staying on as captain when I heard that I had a rival candidate in Piet Keizer, so there was going to be a ballot. People were still complaining that I was too self-serving. It was a form of jealousy I had never before experienced.

In the end, the players chose Piet. It was a terrible shock. I immediately went to my room, phoned Cor Coster and said he needed to find a new club for me straight away. That was it. I had suffered the kind of injury that you can't see with the naked eye. The blow was particularly severe because we weren't just fellow players but also close friends. That was why I really didn't see it coming. I've had the same thing happen with other people as well. People you think you have a special bond with, but in the end you have to let go of.

I later thought about that vote a lot. I wondered what I had done wrong. As a captain I was sociable, but I sometimes had to be antisocial as well. Kovács's 'hands-off' approach forced me to act when I thought our performance was suffering because of it. I had to be critical, both of the group and of individual players. Perhaps that wasn't clever at a time when everyone in our team was admired, but I felt professionally obliged to do it as the captain. However, I always acted with the aim of improving things and never destructively.

That was what led to the biggest confrontations. Telling some of the guys that they had to improve their behaviour. Making it clear to them that yesterday's win was all well and good, but that we wouldn't necessarily win again tomorrow if we didn't put the effort in. Arguments surfaced more and more frequently. I was even more wounded because I felt I'd done a lot for the other players, such as pioneering the Dutch Professional Football Players Union (VVCS). This would later result in the Contractspelers Fonds (CFK), which is, as far as I know, the only pension scheme for footballers in the world.

In the end, my father-in-law and Karel Jansen set up the

VVCS, although I've never been a member. People criticize me for being instrumental in setting the association up and then never joining it. I had to point out that the organization wasn't meant for the likes of me. I already earned a high salary and was in a good position to sort out my own affairs. But the same wasn't true of a lot of other players, certainly in the regional teams. For them, VVCS was a blessing, but it wasn't suitable for me. That's why I didn't have to become a member, so that I still had the possibility of coming down on either the players' side or the administration's if the situation called for it. Also, it's unwise to mix high earners and average earners. You've only got one organization, and it's not a good idea.

I did something similar at Ajax. The club had received a lot of money from playing in the European Cup but, because we'd previously always been knocked out in the early rounds, it was never shared with the players who'd earned it. Eventually, I suggested that 70 per cent should go to the team. Effectively, this wouldn't cost the club a penny because UEFA competition prize money wasn't included in the annual budget. The board didn't want to get involved, even though it was a perfectly honest, performance-related deal. In my view there's not much wrong with receiving a bonus for doing well. In the end I had my way, and the team and the club shared the money.

Given all of this, you can perhaps see why voting me out as captain came as such a blow. Of course, going to Barcelona was a great career move, but it would never have occurred to me if it hadn't been for that incident at training camp.

Why Barcelona? Spain had just opened its borders to foreign players, Rinus Michels had moved there from Ajax two years before, and I'd been to the city on holiday. I'd also met Carles Rexach in Mallorca a few times. He played for Barcelona and had some great stories about the club and the city. They were a proud club at the heart of local life, but when they made an offer for me they hadn't won a league title for over a decade.

I was feeling unsettled and unwanted at Ajax and, in those circumstances, if a club like Barcelona wants you, then you're bound to take a closer look. Especially when the transfer fee will break the world record.

One happy accident was that Vic Buckingham, the man who had given me my debut when he was a trainer at Ajax, had worked at Barcelona before making way for Michels. Armand Carabén, a great guy with a Dutch wife, also happened to be a member of the board. Another few coincidences that I don't consider coincidental. And there was also the fact that the salary on offer was gigantic. At Ajax in those days I was earning a million guilders, on which I paid 72 per cent tax. At Barcelona, not only would I get twice as much, but I'd be paying only 30 or 35 per cent to the Spanish taxman. I wasn't just earning a lot more; I was also getting to keep more of it.

The more I thought about it, the more sense it made. I would be playing football in a southern country, in tough competition with clubs like Real Madrid, which had featured great names like Ferenc Puskás and my old hero Alfredo Di Stéfano. In the end, it was an easy decision to sign. General Franco was in power in Spain at the time, so of course I was criticized for going to play football in a dictatorship. When it was clear that I was leaving Ajax, I was sent all kinds of poisonous messages and lots more of that kind of nonsense. But the worst thing for me was that

Ajax gave my mother, who had always done her best for the club, an inferior seat in the stadium. Behind a pole. That absolutely crushed me.

On 2 December 1968 I had married Danny. From a life in which I'd only had to think about myself and my football, I suddenly had to start sharing things and getting more involved with the people around me. In my case, my new-found responsibility as a family man carried over into football. Almost immediately I began to think more about the rights of other players as well as my own. I started getting involved in things like the bonus system.

I wasn't surprised at the speed of the change: I'd never been one to put off until tomorrow what I could do today. When circumstances changed, I was quick to adapt, and to see things through to the end. At home, I received a lot of support from Danny that helped me to do that. And the more I think about it, the more I come to the conclusion that shaping my family played a part in the origins of Total Football. This was a style of playing that could only be carried out by footballers who could play not just for themselves, but for the rest of the team too. Ten players needed constantly to be aware of what the man with the ball was doing and anticipate what he would do next.

That's exactly what happens in a family, certainly if there are children. Of course, everything one person in a family does affects the others, and my experience as a husband and father proved invaluable when it came to leaving Ajax. Chantal was born in 1970 and Susila came along two years later, so when we moved to Barcelona in 1973 I was right in the middle of my domestic learning process, and well equipped to deal with all the commotion surrounding my transfer. It started as soon as we landed at Barcelona airport. So many people, so much enthusiasm. On the one hand I was intimidated, on the other it was incredibly inspiring. After the negative period with Ajax I was finally absorbing new energy again.

I'd also been given a nice little present by the Royal Dutch Football Association, the KNVB, football's governing body in the Netherlands. In Holland the transfer window ended in July, while in Spain it stayed open until the end of August. So the KNVB refused to grant permission for me to play and I had to wait for two months before Barcelona could use me in a competitive fixture. So a decision was made to organize some friendlies so that the supporters at least had a chance to see me in action. It was a great success. Every game was a sell-out and after only three matches the club had earned back my transfer money.

Of course, the KNVB weren't happy when the friendlies were arranged, but then I threatened to withdraw from the Dutch national team. As the World Cup in Germany approached, the deciding qualifier in Belgium was scheduled for November, and a few more friendly internationals were planned before that. I said that without sufficient match practice I couldn't make myself available for the Oranje. How can you expect someone you force to stand on the sidelines for two months to perform at that level?

The pressure had worked, and on 5 September 1973 I made my debut for Barcelona in a friendly against Cercle Brugge. The score was 6–0, I scored three times and suddenly everyone was convinced that my world record fee was justified. After that we played three more friendly matches – against Kickers, Arsenal and Orense – and won all of them. This was all well and good on the surface, but the impact of the results was all the greater because of

Barcelona's miserable start in the league. When I made my La Liga debut, in a home game against Granada on 28 October, the team had won only a single match and was mired somewhere near the bottom of the league.

Luckily, the Granada match marked a turn in our fortunes. The final score was 4–0, I scored twice and after that we didn't lose a single game, winning the league by eight points. That season I went out on a high. The enthusiasm throughout the club was very inspiring, but at the same time I realized only too clearly that the bar was being set higher every year. Still, as long as I kept performing everything would be fine. However, from the get-go there was always something odd going on in Barcelona. Nothing went to plan. Take the birth of my son, Jordi, in 1974. On Danny's due date, 17 February, there was an away game scheduled against Real Madrid. Except that we'd decided to have our third child in Amsterdam like the others, with the same gynaecologist who had delivered Chantal and Susila, and again by caesarean. And I wanted to be there, as I had been the other two times.

The most natural thing in the world as far as I was concerned, but behind my back everyone seemed to be panicking. Eventually Rinus Michels asked if the operation couldn't be brought forward a week. I'm sure he must already have been talking to the doctor behind my back. Anyway, Danny and I agreed, Jordi was born on 9 February and a week later I was able to play in Madrid. But that turned into a great carry-on as well, since Danny had to wait ten days after the caesarean before she could come home. So, after the Real match, which we went on to win 5–0, I'd immediately flown back to the Netherlands to pick up Danny while everyone in Catalonia was over the moon.

When we touched down at Barcelona airport a few days later with the baby there was another big hoo-ha since the supporters hadn't finished partying. That result in the Bernabéu had an incredible impact, not just on the club, but also on the whole of Catalonia. The region was suffering under the tough regime of the dictator Franco in the capital, so the victory had huge political significance. I discovered that myself when I went to register Jordi in Barcelona.

While Danny had been recovering in hospital, I had recorded Jordi's birth in Amsterdam. (Officially, his full name is Johan Jordi, but he was to be known as Jordi.) I'd brought the Dutch registration papers with me to Barcelona so that I could also register him in Spain, as I was required to do. It was just as well, because I was told by the registrar that Jordi, which is a Catalan name (Sant Jordi is the patron saint of Catalonia), wasn't permitted and that he would therefore have to be registered under the name Jorge, which is the Spanish version.

'Then we've got a problem,' I told the official. 'His name is Jordi, and Jordi it will remain. If you won't do it, then I will take it further, but in that case it'll become your problem.'

My stand had less to do with politics than with our right to determine what our child would be called. Because we hadn't known his sex in advance, the previous December we'd decided on two names: Nuria for a girl and Jordi if it turned out to be a boy. Those names were unheard of in the Netherlands, so Danny and I thought they were pretty special.

As the birth approached and we shared the names with other people in Spain, we were told that we could forget the

Catalan Jordi. I immediately said that Danny and I would decide for ourselves what the child would be called, and it was no one else's call to make. We chose the names because we liked them, not because one of us had a relative called by them. We had already called our first daughter Chantal, which is French. Susila is an Indian name. That was also to do with the attitude of our generation. You sometimes did things that deviated from the rules of the generations that had gone before.

I said that to the official in Barcelona as well. At first he said it was impossible. To which I said that it was his bad luck if it was. The nationalist emotions unleashed by the Real Madrid game must also have been on his mind, and in the end I also gave him a decent excuse to use. Because I'd registered Jordi in Amsterdam first, I was able to show him the Dutch birth certificate and tell him that he couldn't simply overrule an official document. Because whatever he wrote down, the birth certificate would still be valid anywhere in the world. That put his mind at rest, and he registered Jordi without further ado. So the 5–0 win didn't just have great emotional value for the Catalan people; my son also benefited from it at the register office. Because I doubt whether the official would have been so quick to change his mind if we'd lost in Madrid or been somewhere near the bottom of the table.

Rinus Michels had devised a new system for the match against Real, and everything went to plan that evening in Santiago Bernabéu. The tactics that Michels had come up with worked perfectly. In that game I didn't play as an out and out striker, but dropped back a little, meaning that other players could drive into the space that was created. It was a striking tactical move, which had not been used before, but I only found out years later how Michels came up with it. At that time a friend of Michels, Theo de Groot, whom he had once played with at Ajax, was living in Madrid. Theo, father of the sports journalist Jaap de Groot, lived next door to Real centre back Gregorio Benito, who often crossed the corridor to visit his Dutch neighbours. He clearly didn't know anything about the relationship between de Groot and Michels, because before the match against Barcelona he revealed Real's entire game plan. The core strategy was that I wouldn't be man-marked, but instead I would be marked zonally by the Madrid back line.

When Michels learned this he asked me to play deeper. Then the four defenders, with nothing to cover, would get confused and our advancing midfielders would take advantage. The plan worked, our midfielders breaking forward took Real completely by surprise. It's remarkable how chance events can have major consequences. After that 5–0 victory we played a series of matches whose like had never been seen before. Three months later Barcelona were national champions for the first time in fourteen years. It was an unforgettable experience, and one that still gives me a good feeling when I think back on it. Unlike my time at Ajax, my leadership as captain was accepted at Barcelona. As a leader you serve by always taking responsibility. I've always said that having a family helped me in that. It taught me to be more involved with other people. That involvement is also part of Total Football.

During that hectic first season at Barcelona I became better and better at coping with a great deal of pressure, both on and off the field. That was part of the captain's role, of course. Michels helped a lot with that. It was claimed later that I was the one who made him so great, but he was instrumental in my development as a player by always giving me the right advice at the right time. From when I was an eighteen-year-old at Ajax and he singled me out and made me think about match tactics, he always brought a huge amount of professionalism to the context in which I had to perform. Michels picked up the pace and paid constant attention to every detail of our development. Later on, when I became a coach and advisor, I discovered for myself how difficult it is if your players aren't inspired to perform to the maximum. When that happens, however much you want to and however hard you try, you're never going to succeed. Michels created the forwards I needed around me as a player. He did this at both Ajax and Barcelona, and also with the Dutch national team. That isn't to say that my input didn't take things to the next level, but to achieve that you need other people, because you'll never manage to do it on your own.

3

Michels' appointment to replace František Fadrhonc as manager of the Dutch national team for the 1974 World Cup finals in Germany was very important to me. Perhaps even crucial. Of course I hadn't forgotten how I was kicked out of Ajax. I'd met up several times with my former team-mates in the national side, and at first that had really been a problem. Not least because they were still moaning about me. Why did I always seem to arrive later than they did for the internationals? They just didn't realize how long it took to travel from Spain in those days. There weren't the number of flights that there are now.

For example, on one occasion when I played a match in the north of Spain I first had to take the bus back to Barcelona and then fly to Amsterdam, from where I caught a connecting flight to some little spot in the Eastern Bloc where we were due to play a World Cup qualifier. All very complicated: I set off on Sunday and arrived on Tuesday for the Wednesday night match. Then I later discovered that some of the players were annoyed with me for not travelling with the rest of the team. But how could I have done that?

Fadrhonc didn't back me, so this was a bitter pill that I just had to swallow. I sometimes wondered whether it was worth the trouble but, given the prospect of appearing in the World Cup finals for my country, not playing was hardly a realistic option, and no option at all when the KNVB decided to appoint Michels to manage the Dutch side. When he arrived, all the forwards were told to practise what became known during the tournament as Total Football. Total Football requires talented individuals acting in a disciplined group. Someone who whines or doesn't pay attention is a hindrance to the rest, and you need a boss like Michels to nip that in the bud. I don't know who came up with the term 'Total Football', but it gets the meaning across. Total Football is, aside from the quality of the players, mostly a question of distance and positioning. That's the basis of all the tactical thinking. When you've got the distances and the formation right, everything falls into place. It also needs to be very disciplined. You can't have someone striking out on their own. Then it doesn't work. Someone will start to pressurize an opposition player, and then the whole team has to switch gear.

An example. When putting pressure on a right-footed defender, I would close him down on his right, forcing him to pass with his weaker left foot. Meanwhile Johan Neeskens would be coming up from midfield on his left, forcing the opponent to make the pass quickly. That made his problem even worse. To do that, Neeskens had to let his man go. That meant that *his* opponent was unmarked, but that guy couldn't track Neeskens because, from our defence, Wim Suurbier had pushed up to fill Neeskens' position. Quickly and effectively, we'd created a three-on-two situation. So to cut a long story short: I put pressure on the opponent's stronger side, Neeskens did the same on his weak side and Suurbier made sure that Neeskens' marker was forced to hold position. All of that happened within a radius of five to ten metres.

That, in fact, has always been the essence of Total Football, you always play based on what you can see and never on what you can't see. In other words, you always need to have an overview, you always need to be able to see the ball.

Take rugby. The players have to the pass the ball backward to be able to run forward. As a result, they have a better overview of what's happening in front of them. The same theory can be applied to football, but a lot of people don't see it that way. They think they have to play the ball forward, when in fact the man coming up the field from behind is the one they should be playing to. He's in a deeper position, but he has an overview.

At any rate, Total Football has everything to do with distances on the field and between the lines. If you play like that even the goalkeeper counts as one line. Since the keeper can't pick up a back pass, he has to be able to play football with it. Someone who can make sure that the defenders receive the ball at the right moment. He often has to be positioned at the edge of the penalty area, to be an option for the teammates in front of him. In our style of play for the World Cup in Germany there was no room for a keeper who never came off his line.

That was why Jan Jongbloed was chosen over Jan van Beveren, until then our first choice keeper. The great thing was that in his youth Jongbloed had been an attacker. As a goalkeeper he didn't just like joining in, he was also very good at it and often avoided conceding because he was able to think like an attacker. In front of Jongbloed, our defence had only one true defender, Wim Rijsbergen. Arie Haan was a midfielder and the full backs Ruud Krol and Wim Suurbier had originally played further forward. Almost all of them were footballers who could think in terms of the overall game. They were positionally sound and technically even better.

Turning a midfielder or attacker into a defender, of course, dates back to Michels' philosophy at Ajax. It was assumed that someone who had been a winger between the ages of eight and eighteen could always think about what's ahead of him, always look to advance up the field in order to get at the goal as often as possible, even if he was played further back. This implies that he prefers not to run back and benefits from the field staying small. There's also the fact that, generally speaking, midfielders and attackers have better ball skills than a classical defender. That too is an advantage if they're converted.

I've heard and read in various places that people watching that World Cup in Germany thought our way of playing football came about by chance. That's total nonsense. At that time the Dutch national squad comprised a group of players who were terribly good, not just average. Outstandingly good. On the left of midfield you had not only Gerrie Mühren of Ajax, but also Feyenoord's Willem van Hanegem. We had world-class players competing for positions. On the right were Wim Jansen, also from Feyenoord, and Johan Neeskens, who was shortly to leave Ajax to join me at Barça. What more do you want? Just tell me who's the better left winger – Piet Keizer or Rob Rensenbrink? Everywhere you looked there were top-class players who had won trophies in every country they'd played in. Take your pick and they'll do the rest.

It was world-class talent combined with professionalism. Take someone like Ruud Krol, a versatile defender I've always admired enormously. He could play anywhere along the back line and in midfield. Someone who had decided to get to the top and then did his homework to get there. Going back out onto the field after training every day, just to improve his forward passing. Super.

Our starting eleven was just packed with quality, but you could easily have fielded fifteen who were extremely good, and in multiple positions. So the right back could also play at centre half, while either Johnny Rep or René van de Kerkhof could be picked down the right wing. Talented players were everywhere. And they could each bring something extra to the team.

The 1974 World Cup was the culmination of five years of success for Dutch teams at domestic level. It started in 1970 when Feyenoord of Rotterdam beat Glasgow Celtic in the European Cup final, and after that Ajax won it three times in a row. The progress of the Dutch national team to the finals in 1974, the first time they had done so since 1934, was the cherry on the cake. With a team made up mostly of Ajaxers and Feyenoorders, the best of two footballing giants came together at last. The ideal mix.

It was the last big step to the country's recognition as a major footballing nation. It was that summer in Germany that I discovered how big the World Cup really is. With Feyenoord, and above all with Ajax, Dutch football had dominated club competition worldwide for four years, but even that was no match for the aura of a World Cup. The sheer scale of it seemed to influence everything. Just take the impact of the 'Wilhelmus', our national anthem. I'd never heard it being sung so heartily and by so many people before each game. And then all those orange-clad supporters. It was the first time I'd seen so many of them gathered in one place as well. The feeling that you were truly representing your country grew stronger every day. The pride of playing for your country. From players to supporters, everyone was honoured to be part of it.

It got better all the time too, better and better, and soon we had the whole world behind us. There were no mobile phones and internet in those days, so support for the team didn't go viral, but the momentum grew step by step, smoothly building into an almost irresistible force.

The team's preparation for the World Cup, on the other hand, had been anything but smooth. There was a lot of fuss about finance and sponsors. Hardly unexpected, because everything was strange and new to both the players and the KNVB as none of us had experience of a World Cup. Because things were going off in all directions, a players' committee was set up, with representatives from Ajax and Feyenoord, to ensure that we would receive a fair deal. We'd always been rivals on the pitch, but now all of a sudden we were working together to find solutions.

Thanks to my father-in-law, I knew a lot more about things like this than the rest of them. Cor and I were way ahead. The players' committee was also a good opportunity for us to share our experiences with others. We quickly agreed that it wasn't about who earned most, but that it was about the group as a whole. So: sauce for the goose, sauce for the gander. Everyone would get the same retainer and everyone who played would receive a match bonus. The ones who played most matches would get the most money. It was a bit pioneering, but in the end we benefited as a group.

One problem was that I had a sponsorship deal with the sportswear company Puma, which meant that I couldn't wear anything supplied by their competitor Adidas during the World Cup. Until then the Dutch team's kits had carried no logo, but for the World Cup that changed to a shirt bearing the distinctive three stripes that were the Adidas trademark. The KNVB had signed a contract with Adidas without telling the players. They thought they didn't need to because the shirt was theirs. 'But the head sticking out of it is mine,' I told them. In the end, we removed one of the stripes from my shirt, which made it neutral again.

All these off-field organizational things took some getting used to because they were all completely new, but it was also a fantastically brilliant time. Not least because everything would eventually come together. Finding our way also made us stronger. As the tournament approached and after it began, we noticed that we were growing increasingly solid as a group. Although we were all internationals from different clubs, we had become a team. That was apparent during our first match against Uruguay. The team spirit was clear to see. Of course we had self-belief that we could do something brilliant, but in truth we'd never expected that a team from a South American country, one we regarded as a bigger and more established footballing nation, mightn't be able to keep up with us. In fact, we were startled by our own quality. At home, we were used to facing teams who knew exactly how Ajax or Feyenoord played. But this was the World Cup, and our opponents seemed to have not the slightest clue. They were doing things we'd given up doing five or six years ago.

To us, the way we played was entirely natural, but our Total Football was attracting worldwide admiration. Our powerful, dynamic style of play focused on pushing back the opposing team as efficiently as possible, with or without the ball. Defenders could attack and attackers could defend. The aim was that every player should be capable of taking on the ball in the opposition half. People thought it was fantastic to see. It also improved with every match, and that reinforced our feeling that we could be world champions.

Sixteen teams contested that year's World Cup. They were divided into four groups of four, with the group winners and runners-up going on to a second-round stage comprising two groups, A and B. The two second-round group winners would contest the final while the two runners-up would play off for third place.

Apart from the first-round game against Sweden, we won all our group matches by some distance. Uruguay, Bulgaria, East Germany and Argentina, none of them stood a chance. The Sweden game was a 0–0 draw, and as I said immediately afterwards, it's a pity when you fail to produce a positive result after playing so well. But after the match everyone was talking about the feint that I'd done: the so-called 'Cruyff turn', in which, in a forward motion, I drag the ball behind my supporting leg, turn my body away immediately and sprint towards the ball.

The turn wasn't something I'd ever done in training or practised. The idea came to me in a flash, because at that particular moment it was the best solution for the situation I was in. There are impulses that arise because your technical and tactical knowledge has become so great that your legs are able to respond immediately to what your head wants them to do. Even if that's nothing more than a flash in the brain. I've always used feints like that. I've never used them to make the opponent look foolish, only as the best solution to a problem. Yes, I sometimes played the ball through someone's legs, but only if there was no other way of getting past them. That's completely different from nut-megging somebody for fun. That one irritated even me when other people did it.

Both the Netherlands and Brazil – the defending champions – won their opening two second-round matches in Group A, so the last group match between us was, in effect, the World Cup semi-final. For me, that game was the highlight of the tournament. I remember it more clearly than the final. We outclassed the reigning world champions on all fronts. In terms of technique, in terms of speed, in terms of creativity. We were better in every way.

The 2–0 win was a triumph both for the team and for me personally. Not only was my goal, which made it 2–0, later chosen as the best in the tournament, it also symbolized everything that Total Football stood for. Our left winger, Rob Rensenbrink, dropped deep to receive the ball from Ruud Krol, our left back. Rensenbrink then released Krol into the free space and he reached the sideline before crossing for me to score on the volley at the near post. The whole build-up and conclusion are still fantastic to watch.

Even though a lot of people see that game as one of the best in World Cup history, we knew we weren't at our best in the initial phases. Of course, it was Brazil that we were up against. The world champions and, technically speaking, as good as football got. There were all those famous guys playing for them: Jairzinho, Rivellino, Paolo Cézar . . . At first that was part of it, we were a bit star-struck – until we played through it and outclassed them at their own game. Technically, both sides were good, but we were the ones who could up the pace. That was the difference. Our ability to play at speed was much, much better.

The pitch was also an important detail. Brazilian grass

was completely different from European grass. We knew that. You noticed it particularly when you were playing the ball on the ground. In Germany the grass was short, thin and dry, while in Brazil it was longer, thicker and more lush. That has an influence on the speed of the ball; it can make a world of difference. Luckily for us, we were playing in Germany and not in South America, which meant that the surface worked to our advantage.

The Brazilian team was also going through a transitional phase. They were busy leaving pure technique behind, and replacing it with a mixture of technique and physicality. Our foundation was technique and everything else was a matter of positioning and support. Good positional play meant that you didn't have to run so far, so technique was able to come more easily to the fore. In spite of being a bit below par, we did well in the initial phase of the game and went in at half time with the scores level at 0–0. I'd already declared that we were looking forward to Brazil, and in the second half we showed why. We'd been lucky not to concede a few times early in the first half, and after we'd scared ourselves stupid the team rallied to play the best football we could.

Unfortunately, the precise opposite happened in the final against Germany, who were reigning European champions and had Franz Beckenbauer, Gerd Müller and Paul Breitner in their team. Those three and many others in their squad played for Bayern Munich, who were the best team in Europe at the time and had just won the first of three consecutive European Cups. If we'd prepared for them to give as good as they got, as we had against Brazil, it might have worked to our advantage. But after the 2–0 against the world champions everyone was so relaxed and content that the next match didn't seem to matter.

It was a classic case of pride coming before a fall. As soon as you're past that point of over-confidence, it becomes incredibly difficult to turn it round. Against Germany, after a quick opening goal, where we passed the ball between each other something like sixteen times without the Germans touching the ball before they conceded the penalty, we created chance after chance. Then they converted a penalty of their own to level the score at half time, and in the end there was nothing we could do about Gerd Müller's goal that made it 2–1. We thought we were certain to win but, whatever we tried, we just couldn't put the ball in the net again.

Throughout the match everyone was either a bit too early or a bit too late – never on time. It just wasn't quite 100 per cent. Of course you can still play pretty well at 95 per cent, but if your opponents are playing at the top of their game you're in danger of being second best all over the pitch.

Sometimes you can lose a game in your head. Just look at how the goals went in. Wim Jansen making that challenge to give away a penalty and Ruud Krol not keeping his legs together for that second goal. That last one in particular is typical of how we were in that match. A lot of people think that when you're defending you have to boot the ball away every time. But the art of defending is also about understanding when you have to give the goalie a chance to make a save.

What you must never do is let a shot on target slip through your legs. Then there's nothing the goalie can do about it. It's a mistake you see happening every week. The goalie can defend only about five of the seven-metre width of the goal, so as a defender it's your responsibility to screen off the remaining two metres. As soon as you give those two metres away, the goalie is left looking like an idiot. Forwards often wait for the defender to give them an opportunity to shoot through his legs. Four times out of five they'll score, because the goalie is relying on the defender to cover that part of the goal. That's why you must never give space away. It's an aspect of defence that's still very weak in many teams. We never really got going in the final, and Müller's goal proved to be the winner. When it was all over, of course, there was a great feeling of disappointment. You know you're the best in the world, but you haven't won the prize.

That said, I got over it quickly enough. In fact it wasn't that much of a blow. Much more important was the vast amount of positivity and admiration for our play that our performances had generated all over the world. Pretty much everyone who wasn't German thought we should have won. We weren't on top form in the final, but we had set an example for billions of people. We had also given hope to all the players who, like me, weren't big or strong. The whole philosophy of how football should be played was adjusted during that tournament.

That philosophy was actually very simple, and remains so today. There's a ball, and either you've got it or they've got it. If you've got it, they can't score. If you use the ball well, the chance of a good outcome is greater than the chance of a bad one. This shifts the focus to quality and technique, whereas before it was all about effort and hard work.

I experienced the World Cup on a high. The focus was

on me, so I also bore the most responsibility. Luckily I received everyone's support and, to be honest, it all went very easily for me. The press conferences and all that talking is something I've never seen as a nuisance or tiring in any way. In the end you had the guys from the team spontaneously saying to me, 'Keep it short so we can get out of here.'

So all the stories about how I'm supposed to have said after the tournament that this was my last World Cup because it was far too hard – they're all nonsense. That decision came later, and for a totally different reason. During the World Cup I was living in a kind of adrenalin flow, which meant that I didn't feel much stress at all. Don't forget that we were winning a lot of games and suffering no setbacks. Even within the team everything was positive, and it was all a result of the pleasure we experienced from football.

We did have to deal with the gutter press for the first time. Just before the final the German rag *Bild-Zeitung* published photographs and a story about Dutch players and naked German women in our hotel swimming pool. I was supposed to have been there and Danny got to hear about it. They later also managed to get quotes from a few of our second-choice players who had told them that, before the final, I'd had my furious wife on the phone for hours. This was something completely new to me in professional football, the media trying to manipulate a situation. Except it didn't bother me. Even later, as a coach, I seldom or never let publicity influence me, so I certainly wouldn't have done so before playing in a World Cup final. Accusations that we played badly because I was distracted by that story are nonsense. Complete codswallop. As for the story itself, well, Danny was in our second home in the mountains near Andorra, in a place that didn't yet have a phone connection, so we couldn't even have contacted each other on the telephone, let alone argued. It was only after the final that I managed to speak to her, to tell her how this kind of tittle-tattle develops a life of its own.

Sensationalist and inaccurate press coverage is now established as an unfortunate part of the game, but it didn't affect the way we played. The real reasons we lost the final are simple. We missed too many chances, Sepp Maier played the match of his life in the German goal and Germany shouldn't have been given their penalty. Despite losing, and despite the lies in the press, the World Cup is still a beautiful memory for me. Sometimes, even when you don't lift the trophy, in the end you're still seen as a winner. Wherever I go in the world, people always want to talk about our team in those days. I think we earned more praise and respect during that tournament than most world champions before or since. I'm proud of that.

The World Cup turned us into cult figures around the globe. People warmed to our image of gritty bravura. Our strength lay in our honesty. We weren't acting; that was really how we were. Dutchmen by birth, and definitely Amsterdammers by nature.

I also seemed to be a trendsetter. More and more people cared about my appearance, what I wore, how my hair was styled. That was all Danny's influence. She was the one I spent most of my time with. Because, just to be clear, I've never bought my own clothes. I haven't a clue about that sort of thing. I don't notice colours, I don't notice anything at all where clothes are concerned. I just take what's at the front of the wardrobe. I don't even know whether what I'm wearing matches or not. Not a clue. That's why I've never bothered about how I dress. Same with my hair. I let it grow because Danny liked it that way. I couldn't have cared less how I looked. Although I'd been part of many trophy-winning club sides, it was only after that World Cup that I achieved true stardom. Everything I said and thought suddenly mattered. Not just in Holland, but all over the world. It's an impact that still often surprises me.

The 1974 World Cup was not only very special for me, it was also a high point for the nation. Something that started at Ajax in 1965 was crowned in 1974 with the best football that the Netherlands has ever played. Unfortunately, and by definition, after a high point things can only go downhill.

In spite of the fantastic experience of 1974 and my football in the following seasons at Barcelona being of a high standard, I chose not to go to the World Cup Finals in 1978. At first I had my doubts, even though I'd always thought that I would retire from the game in 1978. If you ask me why, I don't have the faintest idea. Stopping when I reached thirty-one had been an idea in my head since I was a boy. That's why I think I might not have been mentally sharp enough to have merited a place in a World Cup squad, knowing that it was over and out afterwards. After the disappointment of the European Championships in 1976, when we went out to Czechoslovakia in a dreadful semi-final, those doubts started growing. My positive feeling came back briefly in 1977. The Dutch team played a few brilliant matches against England and Belgium, and I started seriously wondering whether I should take the opportunity to go to Argentina the following summer with such a strong team.

Then something awful happened. It was 17 September and I was at home in our apartment complex in Barcelona, watching a basketball game on television, when the doorbell was rung by what looked like a courier delivering a parcel. When I opened the door, though, I got a gun pressed against my head and was ordered to lie on my stomach. Everyone was at home. The children were in their room, and the man told Danny to lie on the floor as well.

I tried to talk to him. 'Do you want money? What do you want?' I was tied up and roped to a piece of furniture. To do that, he had to set his gun down briefly, and at that moment Danny got to her feet and ran out of the room, out of the building. The bastard ran after her. I was able to free myself and grabbed his gun to make sure he didn't get hold of it again. There was so much screaming that doors were being opened over the whole complex. He was quickly foiled.

A van with a mattress in it was later discovered outside our flat, so everything pointed to a kidnapping of the kind that was a common occurrence in Spain at the time. I don't know anything about his motive, and I wasn't interested in it. I never tried to find out. Only one thing mattered, and that was that the guy was out of our lives.

The next six months or so was a terrible time. We lived with a permanent police guard. When I travelled, when I took the children to school, when I went to train or play with Barcelona. There were always people with me, people walking around me. There was always a police car nearby or in view or driving behind me. Policemen slept in our sitting room every night. The atmosphere was unbearable.

Impossible. The strain was such that I couldn't take any more. I couldn't even relieve the burden by talking about it. The police just said, over and over again, please don't go on about it, because you might put ideas in the heads of other lunatics.

In a situation like that you don't travel to the other side of the world and leave your family on their own for up to eight weeks, so there was no way that I was going to Argentina with the Dutch team. If you're playing a World Cup you have to be fully focused. If you're not, and you have any distractions or doubts whatsoever, then you shouldn't go. Nothing good will come of it.

Holland's coach Ernst Happel called in on me in Barcelona to discuss my withdrawal, but I didn't waver for a second. Since I'd been ordered to keep quiet about the kidnap attempt, I told Happel that I wasn't in the right physical or mental state to play in such an important tournament. I don't think he was convinced, because a World Cup is on a different level. A great sportsman like Happel felt that to miss such an opportunity wasn't right, but I couldn't give him the full story. Then there was the national 'Pull Cruyff Across the Line' campaign. I was sent postbags full of requests from Dutch fans pleading with me to go with the Oranje and begging me to change my mind. But the safety of my family had to come first, so it wasn't at all hard for me to hold my ground. After the kidnapping attempt, I never had a moment's doubt about not going to Argentina. It was out of the question. Anyone who would leave his family behind in those circumstances would be out of his mind.

Unfortunately the repercussions of the attempted kidnapping continued and we felt threatened for a long time afterwards. A girl was kidnapped in Valencia, and Danny and I also heard that the culprits knew we had children, and they were coming to pay us a visit. So we bought two Dobermann pinschers for our own safety, and the whole family underwent training in how to handle the dogs. The police advised us to get rid of them, 'Because just imagine what would happen if they attacked an intruder.' I replied that that was precisely the point of having them.

In the end, then, I missed the World Cup for several reasons. And, in retrospect, by doing so I lost the chance to end my career at the top. When the Netherlands reached the final again, against the hosts, the BBC invited me to be a pundit for the game. I had a hard time in the studio there. Having been behind since the thirty-eighth minute in a bad-tempered encounter, we were denied a second half penalty, scored a late equalizer and hit the post in the final minute, only to go down 3–1 in extra time.

You watch a game like that and the thought runs through your head that if you'd been there your career might have ended with a world title. If only I'd done this, if only I'd done that. It doesn't happen to me very often, but it really took hold of me that time. A feeling of what I could have achieved had I been there, but knowing full well that I would have had to leave my family behind to achieve it. And I couldn't have done that.

Would we have won it if I could have been there? I think, quite honestly, that we might have done. Because my qualities, even at that point, would still have added value to the team. We'd proved that the previous year at Wembley, where we'd beaten England 2–0 and the next day's headline had been 'A total sight of football delight'. A fantastic sentence that I've never forgotten. I even had the feeling that we were a bit further on as a team than in 1974. I could have joined in, but I chose to get out. Then, at the BBC, I found myself thinking: Damn, I would really have liked to be there. It was all very strange and rather sad.

Because the true story had to stay under wraps, my wife had a rough time again. That ridiculous story about all the phone calls before the 1974 final was followed in 1978 with accusations that Danny was the evil genius behind my refusal to play in Argentina. It's really incredible. If there's ever been a footballer's wife who hasn't sought publicity, then it's Danny. But she was blamed for pretty much everything. I kept quiet about all this for decades, but the rumours and accusations continued to be dragged out regularly. It was like our family was constantly receiving a slap in the face. After nearly thirty years, once all the children had left home, I decided to reveal the truth. And that was that. That was that for good. But even after all those years I'm still always on the alert, wherever I am, in case the press is eavesdropping. I've even developed a phobia about opening my mouth in my house. I've had to learn to deal with that kind of thing, that's how it has to be.

4

I played for Barcelona for five years, from 1973 to 1978. That gave me a bond with the club, and also with the Catalans. That was reinforced ten years later when I became coach with Barcelona and our family moved to Catalonia for good. The first season as a player I described earlier was spectacular, of course. The huge excitement about my arrival, the 5–0 win at Real Madrid, the championship and then, for me personally, the World Cup in Germany. Expectations in and around Barcelona always ran high, but after 1974 we didn't win the championship again while I was there. We didn't win the Copa del Rey until my final season.

The longer I played in Spain, the more I understood how important a part politics played in the game. At first I was never one to toe the party line like the other players. Not me. I'm an Amsterdammer who tells it like it is. In the days of General Franco's regime and its immediate aftermath that was still unusual in Spain. Armand Carabén, a Catalan nationalist who was a member of the Barcelona board at the time, thought my attitude was great. I didn't give that too much thought at the time, but later on I understood that he deliberately used my character as part of the club's contribution to Catalonia's escalating struggle for freedom against the powers in Madrid. As an internationally famous foreign player I was completely untouchable, which meant that Franco could be provoked from time to time.

At first, I wasn't really aware of what he was doing. I was playing football, not politics. But eventually I noticed that things weren't working out as well as they ought to have been. Obviously it's crazy that I was part of a championship-winning side only once in five years. In 1977 in particular we were robbed. I was in the best form of my life, and everything pointed to us winning the title. Then, for no good reason, I was suddenly sent off in a match against Málaga. According to the ref I'd called him 'hijo de puta', meaning son of a bitch. But to this very day I've never said any such thing. Not then, and not afterwards. I did talk a lot on the field, but that was mostly when I was coaching or cajoling my teammates. Of course, in the heat of action I sometimes called out things that weren't entirely polite, but we were playing top-level football, and sometimes you have to be harsh to be clear. Even so, I've never abused people with insults like son of a bitch. I think 'nutcase' is about as bad as I got.

In the game against Málaga, I shouted something to one of my teammates who had lost his man a few times. Something like, 'You've got to cover your man.' When the ref came up to me and sent me off the field, I was flabbergasted. That wasn't right. Unfortunately, it happened, and later, in front of the disciplinary committee in Madrid, it was his word against mine. I hadn't a hope and was suspended for three matches, two of which we lost and one of which was a draw. After that, we could whistle for the championship. Atlético Madrid won La Liga that season, interrupting a five-year winning sequence for their city rivals Real. Even today that sending off is the clearest proof to me of how much politics influenced the competition in those days. Luckily a lot of things have changed in Spain since then, and since the transition to democracy in around 1980 Barcelona have won fifteen titles against Real Madrid's twelve.

Life as a player with Barcelona was amazing. As a place to live Barcelona was brilliant. Just fantastic. And the presence of Rinus Michels and Johan Neeskens, who had been bought from Ajax after me, made sure that we never completely lost the Dutch flavour. Sadly, I was never really able to fully enjoy my time in Spain with my family, because football took up every waking hour. In particular I found travelling to away games a trial, often by bus or train and sometimes at night, which meant that we had to sleep on the journey. I was travelling a lot and hardly ever at home; sometimes it was really gruelling.

Rinus Michels was the trainer when I went to Barcelona, but he wasn't the man who brought me to the club. Armand Carabén told me later that the Bundesliga's top scorer, Gerd Müller, had been Michels' first choice. I never talked to him about it and, equally, he never did anything to imply that I was second best, and just as he had at Ajax, at Barça he discussed everything with me in advance, and put me in charge on the field. That wasn't the case with Hennes Weisweiler, who replaced Michels as coach before the 1975–76 season. I rarely had an argument with any other trainer, but he's the only one I couldn't work with. The problem with Weisweiler was mostly that he was always telling adults what they needed to do, regardless of their ability to do it. That works if a player possesses the requisite skills, but he didn't seem to take that into account. It left some players completely stuck.

Eventually I said to him: 'What are you up to? You're

telling players to do things they're absolutely incapable of.' Weisweiler was furious, and couldn't understand my attitude. It was typical of the gulf between German and Dutch training methods. In those days, in Germany, the trainer made the decisions and everyone else obeyed them. In Holland we were about collaborative effort. When we all agreed on something, then we did it, and if we couldn't agree, then we didn't. That season we finished second to Real Madrid. Before the end of it, Weisweiler was sacked and he blamed me for it. But if he'd looked in a mirror he'd have known that it wasn't just me his method didn't work on, it didn't work on anyone in the team. Weisweiler and Barcelona was a combination that was doomed to fail. As happens far too often, it was a question of the wrong trainer at the wrong club.

When I decided to retire in 1978, my two farewell matches for my previous clubs were an omen that my career wasn't destined to end that way. In Barcelona we lost 1–3 to Ajax, and the game organized later in Amsterdam against Bayern Munich was a car crash in which we were slaughtered 8–0. Not exactly the kind of farewell you dream of. After that I became a businessman. That decision was one of the most important lessons in my life, perhaps the most important.

It happened during a time when things were a bit out of control. I only saw my father-in-law three or four times a year. When I was still playing football, Cor didn't have all that much to do as my agent. I had contracts that lasted for several years, the terms were all agreed and I spent 80 per cent or more of my time training or playing football. But from the moment I stopped playing, that 80 per cent was spent in other ways. I also began to use the pig-headedness that had served me so well in football in completely the wrong way.

I shan't name names here, but let me just say that during the course of my career I'd built up a circle of acquaintances, one of whom came up with an investment suggestion that sounded great. Unfortunately, it was in an area of business I knew nothing about, plus – and this is the stupidest thing – something I actually had absolutely no connection with. My ignorance was being exploited. I had money, and where there's money you'll find rats running about. You know that, and now so do I. But I didn't know it then.

Believe it or not, I invested in a pig-breeding venture. How on earth did I get involved in *that* . . . ? If you enjoy doing something, or you have an interest in something, then you can perhaps explain investing in it. But there was no explaining this. I just dived in. I didn't even tell Danny what I was doing. Sometimes you don't realize how foolish you're being until someone points out that you're deluding yourself. Someone asks you, 'What in God's name are you doing? Is this your future? The way you want to spend the rest of your life?' Then you honestly have to admit your mistake. That you're really not interested in pigs at all. That you're banging your head against a brick wall. So hard that you've got no excuses left.

For a little while I thought I was on to a good thing, until my father-in-law visited us in Barcelona again. 'What have you done?' he demanded. I told him I'd bought three plots of land that we could build on. Cor immediately asked to see the deeds to the land. Then he tore into me. I'd paid, but I'd never asked to see any papers. I wasn't used to that kind of thing.

To cut a long story short, it seemed there were no deeds.

Cor said I'd been shafted. 'You've paid for it, but there is nothing in your name.' There was nothing I could do. Cor was very firm, and he said to me, 'Get that whole business out of your head. Accept your losses and then go and do what you're good at.'

That was bad enough, but on top of everything there came Josep Lluís Núñez. In 1978 he became president of Barcelona and immediately pulled a fast one on me, the first of many. For years, the clubs in Spain had paid the players' taxes. At some point the law was changed and everyone had to pay up retrospectively. The club said they would meet all the players' liability – except mine. Because I was about to leave Barcelona, Núñez refused to pay on my behalf, even though it was money that I'd earned as a player with the club. Because he needed the rest of the team for the new season he solved the problem for them, but I wasn't going to be there, so had to fend for myself.

I have no idea how much money I lost altogether at the time. Not a clue. Most of my property went. In March 1979 our flat was repossessed and we had to pack our belongings and leave. Newspaper articles appeared in the paper putting my losses in the region of six million dollars, but I don't know whether that's right. What I do know is that it was a lot of money.

I soon pulled myself together again. It wasn't as difficult as it might have been, because I have never been concerned with money. My father-in-law always looked after the finances. When he died in 2008, I had to go to the bank myself for the first time in thirty years. I didn't even know which bank I was with. I have always avoided contact with business matters.

Even if you were to ask me right now how much money

I have, I wouldn't be able to tell you. Not a clue. Let me know if there are any problems. I don't live in that world. It's not my thing. After my one blunder I never invested in anything again. Not a flat, not a plot of land, nothing at all. I know I have money, and that it has been in the bank for years, but I have no idea how much interest I earn, or if I receive any return at all. That might sound a bit stupid, but I'm not even slightly interested. These days a nephew takes care of my banking matters, and lets me know in good time if anything comes up that I should know about.

Being the person I am, the mistakes I made back then were quickly out of my system. Not least because I believe that everyone has a *destino*, a fate of his or her own. Mine was probably to leave the game at a young age, do something phenomenally stupid, and then find my feet as a footballer again. In fact that's the whole story of my playing career in three lines.

Having retired at thirty-one, I was still young enough to put things right by going back to work playing football. Imagine if I'd made the same mistake at the age of thirty-six, then I wouldn't have been able to pick up the thread and play football again. But at thirty-one I could do so quite easily if I had to. And some of the best experiences of my life came after my thirty-second birthday. If I hadn't made those mistakes, I'd have missed out on some fantastic things.

That's why I believe that what actually happened was preordained. I found out when it was too late to save my money, but just in time to continue playing. Where problems are concerned, I've always been very practical. If I can't rectify something, I just switch it off. Start again, new page. I just file setbacks away. Whether it's losing a World Cup final or millions of dollars, I immediately go in search of the positive. I don't know if it's a kind of self-protection, but that's how I am. Some people see it as short-sightedness, others as a survival instinct. Good or bad, I think all experience is terrific. No one starts anything with a view to getting it wrong. Hindsight is wonderful, but it doesn't change a thing. It's far better to learn from your mistakes. My brief career as a businessman was a one-off. After it, as far as I was concerned, it was: 'Great, guys, that one's done, night-night and off we go to the next situation.'

It also gave me an excellent reason to reconsider my decision to stop playing football. How else could I have bounced back? And, in the end, I also realized it might not have been such a good idea to abandon the unique talent I'd been given at such an early age. Thirty-one was just too young, but I'd been given the chance to make amends. Since then I've known my place. It's in football and nowhere else.

I've always said, if you're going to start over, do it well, and that's what I tried to do. After the flat in Barcelona was repossessed, we decided to restart our lives in America. During the six months since I'd given up playing, all kinds of things had been running through my head. All the reasons why I'd played football – pride, passion, camaraderie – were suddenly gone. But it didn't cause tension at home. That was because Danny has always shared in solving our problems. Even when I made those investments without her knowledge, and while bringing up our three children even as our lives were made insecure by the constant threat of kidnapping.

On top of that she was better at dealing with her father

than I was. Of course, I'd made huge mistakes, but Cor also tended to exaggerate the problems a bit. During that kind of discussion with her father, Danny tried to strike a balance. The way she always has. She is also great at organizing things, and I am always involved. In one area we've always been pretty much the same, and that's drawing a line under things and not looking back.

I opted for America in order to make a completely new start. Far away from the past and an ideal place to build something big out of a situation in which I'd gone from a hundred to zero. It was one of the best decisions I ever made. America was where I discovered new ambitions and how to develop them. I signed up with the Los Angeles Aztecs in the North American Soccer League (NASL). There were all sorts of stories doing the rounds that I was in discussion with the New York Cosmos, but that was never on the cards – at least, not as far as I was concerned – because I really didn't want to play on artificial grass. That was fine for baseball and American football, which they play with their hands. American artificial grass was for running on, not playing real football.

I did play one demo game with the Cosmos, however, in which Franz Beckenbauer, who was under contract to them, also played. I also talked to the Ertegun brothers, Ahmet and Nesuhi, the big bosses at Atlantic Records who owned the club. We talked, but there were never any detailed negotiations. The Giants Stadium was beautiful and impressive, but after I'd played once on AstroTurf, I'd had enough.

Artificial grass then was nothing like artificial grass today. It was a kind of carpet, which meant that you sometimes got enormous blisters on the soles of your feet. The ball also rebounded from it in a way that I wasn't used to. The Americans thought it was fantastic, but as far as I was concerned it was out of the question to play football on a mat. I did want to play professionally in America, but only for a team with a grass pitch. So I found myself in the right place with the Aztecs, where there was magnificent green grass in the Rose Bowl. The same thing was true of the Washington Diplomats, the other club I played for in the NASL. When I made my initial choice for the Aztecs the fact that Rinus Michels was the trainer there was also a factor. So after seven months of idleness I was able to pick up the thread again.

The negotiations were carried out in a typically American way. Everything was done at fantastic speed. It was all sorted out within a single day, and I learned that I had a flight from Spain booked in five hours' time, because they wanted me to turn out for them that evening. It's incredible, but true: after a twelve-hour journey, I was on the field four hours after landing. And until the moment when I saw Michels in the changing room I had had no contact with my new manager regarding my transfer to the club.

In the end I played about three-quarters of the game. I scored two goals and that was enough to convince people I would be a good signing. The other great thing is that Michels himself came along to the hotel after the match to give me a massage. I couldn't run any more, and he'd seen that. Apparently, during his training as a sports coach, he had also learned massage, and he was excellent at it. That was the strange thing about Michels: he was always extremely strict and at the same time always extremely caring.

America really was a blank slate. Everyone who'd been

laughing at my misfortunes was far away in Europe, and I found my place in a completely new world. A new world, but one with the same expectations. All kinds of things were going on, so I wasn't bored for a moment. And, of course, we had some great holidays in Hawaii, which was only a five-hour flight from Los Angeles. Less great was the sale of the Aztecs to Mexican investors Televisa Corp. Just like that, the Mexicans wanted to turn it into a Latin American enclave, so I didn't fit with their vision for the club. The owner of the Washington Diplomats came knocking and, almost immediately, I was sold on.

I'd made no transfer request, nor been asked if I wanted to leave, or where I wanted to go. That's the way it worked in the North American Soccer League. I had no contract with the club, just with the NASL. The league itself. You could arrive for training and find out you'd been sold to another club and had to be on the other side of America within forty-eight hours. You just had to take the plane, whoever you were. In those days there was no such thing as a free agent. There was a 'cut and trade' provision that came into effect halfway through the season. If you were injured during that phase there was the risk of your contract being cancelled. The club-as-family aspect of the game that we had in Europe didn't exist. It was all business. The mentality was a long way from what we were used to. Either you were halfway good and you could go on playing, or you were out and they took on someone new.

My idea how of gentlemen's agreements in football should work also originated in the experiences I had in America – such as how clubs might agree on limiting the number of foreign players per team, or reaching a consensus on how to develop youth players collectively, in ways that could be sealed with a handshake and aim for a better balance between teams. Helping each other to maintain a high level of performance. Within American sport they understand more than anyone else how important it is to collaborate. That's also a big difference between the American franchises and a lot of European clubs. In Europe, everyone is out for themselves; no one has the right mentality to raise the game itself to the highest level possible, while at a franchise that's a prerequisite. Americans want and expect the best.

So after the Mexicans moved in, I moved out, right to the other side of America. I wasn't at all keen on the idea. It was March and I was walking around LA in shorts, while there was still two feet of snow in DC. But during my first visit I was completely won over. I got to see all kinds of great things and in the end I was happy with the move. In retrospect, I had two fantastic years there. Washington is unique. Everyone who goes there is only passing through, and no one I met seemed to have been born there. And everything there is politics. So, because the chairman of the Diplomats was a Democrat, I was embraced by the party. The wives of the Kennedys tried to find a house for me, because what I couldn't get my head around at first was that I seemed to be a famous person.

My neighbour was Robert McNamara, who had been Secretary of Defense under John F. Kennedy and in my time was the president of the World Bank. He was a man with an incredible reputation in world politics. I would see him running in the park in his shorts at five o'clock in the morning, and at seven a limousine with American flags flying would stop outside his door. But at the same time he was a really great guy, who gave us all kinds of useful tips

The Ajax Youth Team, circa 1960. Cruyff is in the front row, second from right.

Sent off playing for Holland against Hungary in 1967 – the referee ignored the fact that Cruyff had been kicked all night by the opposition.

Marrying Danny in 1968 – family was always the most important thing in his life.

With Danny and his parents-in-law in 1968.

Cor Coster would be Cruyff's financial guide throughout his career.

Playing for Ajax in 1970 – Total Football had yet to become the finished article.

In 1973 Ajax beat Juventus 1–0 to win the European Cup for the third time in a row.
Dutch football was becoming the benchmark for how the game would be played.

In 1973 Cruyff signed for Barcelona for a record fee. When he arrived, they were hovering above the relegation zone, but by the end of the season Barcelona won La Liga for the first time in fourteen years and Cruyff was crowned European Footballer of the Year.

At Barcelona Cruyff was re-united with Rinus Michels, the former Ajax coach and one of the principal architects of Total Football. Cruyff played for Barcelona from 1973–78.

The 2-0 victory over Brazil in the 1974 World Cup semi-final summed up the philosophy of Total Football.

The pride before the fall: In the 1974 World Cup Final Holland made sixteen passes from the kick-off before going up 1–0. West Germany won the game and the World Cup Final 2–1.

In November 1978 Cruyff waved goodbye to European Football at Ajax before setting off for a new life in America at the age of thirty-two. He was crowned European Player of the Year three times, more than any other player until Lionel Messi.

In 1978, after a disastrous investment in pig-farming almost left him in financial ruin, Cruyff moved to the US to restart his career, signing up with the Los Angeles Aztecs. He's pictured here with Pele and Franz Beckenbauer standing behind him.

From the Los Angeles Aztecs Cruyff moved to the Washington Diplomats, where he first got the idea of starting the Cruyff Foundation. Here he is coaching a young boy at the club's football clinic.

about the neighbourhood. Like where would be a good school for the children and the best places to buy bread and vegetables. Meanwhile, I cycled to training. Because of the beautiful surroundings, and because cycling there was so great.

Washington is an extreme world, but it's really nice. And instructive. For example, the Washington Diplomats were part of the company that also owned Madison Square Garden in New York. Andy Dolich, our general manager, had been trained at the Garden, and the way he ran the Diplomats was an eye-opener to me. I wasn't at all surprised when Andy later went on to win the World Series with the Oakland A's baseball club, and also did very well with the Golden State Warriors, the Memphis Grizzlies and the San Francisco 49ers. So, someone capable of working at the highest level in baseball, basketball and American football was my mentor at the Washington Diplomats. Thanks to my experiences with people like Dolich I know the football sector from soup to nuts. I know what a player thinks, I know what a coach thinks, I know what the sponsors think and I know all the pros and cons of those three elements coming together.

In Washington I got another glimpse of sport at the highest level, because America is about top-level sport. The top-level way of thinking is in their genes. The big difference between America and Europe is that in America sport is regulated by a school system, and in Europe it's done via a club system. In Europe you first have to be scouted by a club in order to progress, while in the USA sport is so important that it's part of the core curriculum. Everyone goes to school, so everyone has a chance. This is a big contrast with the situation on our side of the Atlantic, in which sport and school work are completely separate disciplines. In Europe, schooling is one thing, sport is something else. That's an error. They're the same, except that in sport you learn on a different level. In America they've worked that one out really well. A kid might equally well grow up to become a doctor, a lawyer or an American footballer. They're not career paths that are kept separate from each other, they belong together. Among the Americans, studying and sport are two sides of the same coin. We split them up, they bring them together. That's why, in America, a real Einstein understands sport, and a real sportsman understands Einstein.

In Europe the sportsmen are too often seen as being a bit thick. Of course that's not how it is. You can't be a top sportsman unless you're intelligent. It's impossible. Recently I heard a great story from a friend about a discussion he'd had with the Chinese basketball star Yao Ming, who used to play for the Houston Rockets. At one point they were talking about the best player Yao Ming had ever been up against. Yao thought it was Shaquille O'Neal.

I found the explanation that he gave for that both beautiful and quite special. With Yao Ming, O'Neal found himself dealing with a player who was physically his equal. Same height, same strength. Yao Ming won the ball from him on the first two occasions, but after that he didn't get near it. According to Yao, every attacker in basketball has a hundred situations under the basket that he's experienced before, stored in his head like a list numbered 1 to 100. As a result, during any play he intuitively knows what he's got to do by calling up the right number.

But O'Neal was up against something new in Yao Ming. He'd never played against anyone like him before. Nevertheless, O'Neal seemed able to analyse the new situations almost instantly, and to add them to the database in his head. So within five minutes he had variants 101 and 102 in his system, and was the boss of Yao Ming. Stupid sportsmen can't do that, only very intelligent ones. I myself always say you play football with your head; you just use your legs to run.

If you look at sport and intelligence in those terms, you get a much wider view of how sport and society interact. And you find yourself resisting the narrow-mindedness that persists in a lot of European sport. Of course, America has many more sporting opportunities, but it's also a lot harder to take advantage of them precisely because there are so many. Where we have five players competing for one position in the field, they have five hundred. So the internal struggle is harder, and that inevitably creates a different mentality.

Americans also attach a great deal of importance to data and statistics. Percentages related to what happened and what didn't happen. Perhaps a basketball player who scores with 80 per cent of his shots is bad and one who scores 90 per cent is good. I think that's a debatable way to assess performance. What I know for certain is that the conclusions I would draw from experience are different from the ones based only on figures. Because if Lionel Messi scores three times out of every ten attempts, he might be criticized by someone who sees only the statistics for being just 30 per cent effective. I'd say: just copy him and see if you can get up to that level. It's practically impossible.

Billy Beane was the first one to see that. The top man from baseball's Oakland Athletics looked at the statistics in a different way and recorded surprising successes. He understood that the devil is probably in the detail, but that you also had to be good at seeing that detail in the first place. Then the truth doesn't have to be in the big figures – 70 per cent of matches won, for example – but also in the small ones, the 1 or 2 per cent of brilliance or error that can make all the difference. It's all about how you look at it. It's hardly ever the big mistakes or grandstand moments that are decisive, but the small slips or deft touches. They're the ones you've got to try to minimize or make the most of. So as far as I'm concerned, data and statistics can never take precedence over performance. They're an aid, but you have to look through your own eyes. Beane was the first to understand that, and the great thing is that he was inspired by the Total Football played by the Dutch team at the World Cup in 1974. He was fascinated by the fact that the left back was also able to play as a right midfielder; that so-called specialists were also good in other positions. As a result of that he began to analyse baseball players in a different way.

In America, I also noticed that the primary aim of top-level sport is to entertain the public. I've always said that's how it should be, but it was great to see that, in what is perhaps the greatest sporting country in the world, that's exactly how they think. Spectators work hard all week. When they leave the stadium after the match they have to go home happy and be satisfied with what they've seen. That can happen in many ways. You can win, you can show commitment, but you're not necessarily going to be successful. Thus, you must also learn to relativize. It's a cliché, but winning isn't everything. I've always devoutly believed that. Of course, you always try to win, but what's more important is how you go about doing it. You've got to have a good idea of what your public expects and adapt to it. In America they know that better than anywhere. They know what the fans want to see on the pitch, they know what they want to buy, they know what they want to drink, they know what they want to eat, they know everything.

That applies to soccer too, even though in my time in the NASL I encountered a world of extremes. On the one hand I had to perform at the top level within a professionally run organization; on the other I fronted a television programme in which I first had to explain to viewers how big the pitch was, that the pitch was green and what the lines were for. Football was still new, and had to be explained to many Americans from scratch. In my programme I explained how to kick a ball and where the points of interest were likely to be during the match. It was actually very funny: I was playing at the highest level, but at the same time it was like I was in a children's playground. But it worked. Washington was full of Italians, most of whom loved football. The English there, too, filled the Americans around them with enthusiasm for the game. In fact there were loads of people in America who either were or had once been involved with football, but they needed someone who could do it on television.

Why me? Simply because, in America, you get lots of opportunities if you're famous, and one of the opportunities I got was to have my own television programme. Right place, right time. The Italian and English coaches couldn't have been happier. All of a sudden football was on television, and if something was on TV then it must be important. There were even televised training courses. More and more people joined in and the game's popularity snowballed. It was nice to be a part of that.

In Washington I also had the first experiences that later led me to set up my foundation. I mentioned earlier that the owner of the club was a Democrat, and through him I came into contact with the Kennedy family. At one point I was asked by John F. Kennedy's sister, Eunice Kennedy Shriver, to become an ambassador for the Special Olympics. She had set up the organization for disabled athletes which is now internationally famous. I also felt honoured when I opened the Special Olympics in Poland with her a few years ago.

The seed for my foundation was planted in my first season with the Washington Diplomats. As part of my job, I was doing something that ended up being one of those things so worthwhile that you would have done it anyway. But in all honesty, I can't take all the credit. When I joined Washington Diplomats I was told that, at every away game, I would have to run a training session for disabled children. At first I found that very hard. After a few months I said I wanted to give it up because it was absolutely pointless. Every time I told them to kick a ball one way they fired it off in the opposite direction.

When I told the organizers that, they asked me to watch a video that they'd made of me taking a session. They told me to forget about where the ball landed, but instead to look at the eyes of the child, the eyes of the mother and the eyes of the father. And to see the happiness that I was giving them when they had simply kicked the ball, something they had never managed to do before. Of course, it would take a long time for them to get even slightly better at football, but that wasn't what it was about. It was about them kicking a ball and trying to improve their coordination. The organizers added: 'When you come back next time you'll see a completely different child and a completely different person. You'll see the happiness that they've achieved just by being able to touch the ball with their feet.'

That explanation really opened my eyes. Suddenly I discovered the happiness I'd put in motion. I started to enjoy those sessions; I began to see things differently, and think differently too. Instead of frustration, I was now experiencing enormous satisfaction from the things I was doing. I saw that I was actually doing very little, but big things were happening anyway. For example, a neighbour's little boy had Down's Syndrome. All of a sudden he came walking into my garden with a ball. I taught him to shoot, to head a bit, a bit of this and a bit of that. That went on for a month or two. Until one day I came back from a trip and he was playing football with the other kids in the street. When he saw me he ran over, jumped into my arms and we gave each other two kisses. He was so happy that he could join in the game with the others. Or rather, they let him join in. But the simple fact that he was able to join in at all gave me an incredible amount of confidence that I was doing something good.

That affected other areas, too. In hot weather the boy's family always had to pay special attention. They had a swimming pool, and they were terrified that one day their son, who couldn't swim, would fall into it and drown. One day I was in that swimming pool myself, and as soon as he saw me he took a run and jumped in. He seemed to have lost his fear. The confidence he'd got from playing football had helped him overcome his fear of water, so now he could learn to swim.

I realized then that by helping a little, a bit of this and a bit of that, you can change a child's life. That the return is so high, and for so little effort. That was a life lesson I was able to take to its conclusion with the Special Olympics after football. That's why I have a bit of a problem with people who go on about how winning is the holy grail of professional sport. Of course, the result is important, but the most important thing is the fans: the people who feel the club flowing in their blood. You've got to give them the good feeling too. Some might take issue, but where all that's concerned I'm a very idealistic professional who knows what he's talking about. As a kid I grew up with Ajax. I've left the club three times after different rows but, as a fan, I'm always happy when the club does well. That feeling's in the blood. It's completely indefinable, but the best thing there is.

Almost thirty-five years later, America are ranked among the top twenty-five sides in the world, and the stadiums are getting fuller and fuller for domestic league games. It doesn't surprise me. The Americans are capable of working towards success. They're capable of recognizing their shortcomings and striving to rectify them, because success is what they're after. Of course, there are drawbacks to this mentality. Jürgen Klinsmann, coach of the US national side since 2011, often couldn't select the best possible team because he was obliged to include someone from each franchise. He couldn't take four players from one club, for example. Because every franchise contributes to the national budget, they each need to be able to present an international to their own fans. I don't know whether that's still the case, but I do know that it's very restrictive if you're a coach, and something that would delay the national side's development by years if it were to continue.

In America, sport is an integral part of the education

system. That stimulates still more children to play, which means that participation increases and the pool from which the franchises can do their fishing becomes bigger as well. By now, of course, all the American teams are really strong. Against either the national side or the best clubs in Major League Soccer, any team in the world would have their hands full. There's no shortage of good players these days. That said, they're not yet super strong. The exceptional isn't there yet. That kind of talent can make all the difference.

It has to do with how things are organized at the top. It's about training, it's about coaching and it's about match tactics. Because that one special talent, which is bound to appear eventually, needs to be nurtured. I think that's the biggest shortcoming in the American system, that the exceptions don't yet prove the rule. And not just in football. If you take golf or horse-riding, everyone's doing the same thing. They follow the rulebook to the letter. You keep finding that in day-to-day life. A lot of rules and regulations, but where's your Einstein? Your maverick? If American football can get more flexible about these things, one important obstacle to success will be taken away.

Overall, though, I learned a lot in America. Lessons that I've later been able to adapt to my personal life. We'd just moved into our house in Washington when someone from the club called, anxious to know what sort of liability insurance we'd taken out. I thought: liability for what? I found out that you need insurance even for your front doorstep. Because if someone slips on it and you find yourself up before the judge, you've got a problem. I couldn't believe my ears. Then I was told that someone could claim that there was a banana skin on my step, even if I'd no idea it was there. That he could take a picture after putting a banana skin down himself. 'You've really got to bear all these things in mind,' he said.

Then you start changing your way of thinking. Not just shrugging and refusing to take the crazy message seriously, but changing gear mentally and accepting the situation for what it is. In the end I said to the man, 'Fine, it would be great if you could sort that out for us.' I could have made some smart comment about his country's legal system but, the way I saw it, it was actually very special that the club was busy trying to anticipate problems even at that level. You shouldn't laugh, just have a lot of respect.

It's also one of the things that isn't regulated well in Europe. Here we rarely or never spend time anticipating problems. Hence all the fuss about footballers who come from a poor family, play good football, get rich and go off the rails. Put yourself in their position. Just try to digest it. In fact, hardly any European clubs even look at that kind of issue. Because the worlds are too far apart. The board, the directors and the managers who should be keeping an eye on things like that don't understand the culture of players from that sort of background. They just don't have the life experience to be able to imagine themselves in that situation. Who's going to mentor them, who's going to put them on the right track? We've still got a long way to go in Europe where that's concerned.

America gave me three beautiful, instructive seasons with the Aztecs and the Diplomats, during which I was able to take stock of my life. It was also an enormously rewarding time. I was made an honorary citizen of Los Angeles by the mayor, Tom Bradley, and an honorary member of the board of Special Olympics North America. At the same time I learned a great deal about managing a professional organization. Working with specialists, in an environment in which everyone's aim is to improve the performance of the team, from the ticket salespeople to the equipment manager.

It was also in America that I started thinking about setting up what would later become my foundation and my schools. I began putting out feelers for things that I would put into effect fifteen years later, thanks to my experience with the Special Olympics and the way in which study and sport fit together in America. Even today I'm still a bit proud to have been one of those people, along with Pelé, Franz Beckenbauer, Johan Neeskens and all the rest, who pioneered the rise of football in that still-developing continent. When I see how soccer is improving there, I know it's just a matter of time before an American team wins the World Cup. As a football lover, I'd think that was great.

5

Since I stopped playing there in 1981, I've been back to America many times. It's an interesting and inspiring country, certainly where sport is concerned, and in my three years there I learned everything I could from their system, thought about a lot of things and went into action as a player again at a competitive level. They were great years, but it wasn't enough for me as a footballer. I wanted more, and I had more to give. That feeling was only reinforced when I was training with Ajax during the American off-season. I could still hold my own against Eredivisie first-team regulars, and so I decided to take that step again. Back to Dutch football. After a brief spell with Levante in Spain, I made up my mind to return to Amsterdam.

Playing for Ajax again was fantastic. They were a young squad, and they were looking forward to playing alongside me. But I quickly ran into a problem. In America I'd become used to how they manage clubs over there. So, as far as I was concerned, effective football no longer just meant playing well on the field, it also meant looking at how people were running the club. And why they were doing it. And off the field, I wasn't pleased by what I saw.

Luckily, on the field Ajax was still Ajax. They'd won the title in 1979–80 and the squad included a lot of young players. I was thirty-four when I rejoined as a player, and got on well with many of the young guys. Frank Rijkaard,

Marco van Basten; I was suddenly a leader, in every respect. First of all as a footballer, I had to be convincing from day one. I had something to prove. Everyone was talking about the old prick who'd come back. That's what we're like in Holland, seeing the negative side. But I was lucky enough to score early in our match against Haarlem. A good one too. Everyone's jaws dropped again. The critics had to shut up, because I still seemed to have what it took.

After that I spent most of my time on the pitch as cover for other players, which in fact was why I'd been signed. By that stage of my career I'd played in pretty much every position except in goal. Striker, midfielder, sweeper, I'd done it all. As far as that was concerned, nothing was new to me. But I was dealing with a new generation of footballers who had things sorted out for them that we'd had to do for ourselves ten or twelve years before. The conventions and habits they had grown up with were logical within themselves, but as a top footballer you have to go on thinking. You have to go on improvising. If you've got that when you go out on the pitch, you take it with you into the game.

I'm talking here mostly about the social aspect. The certainties. My mother and then my wife still had to wash my muddy kit, but those guys had their kits laid out for them in the changing room in the morning. We didn't have a nice old auntie who had coffee, fresh juice, sandwiches and pasta ready in the player's home. There was nothing. Absolutely nothing. What I saw when I came back to Ajax was a pattern of habits of an easier life and less responsibility. Players who cleaned their own boots? I didn't see them. So guys would roll up during the warm-up and say with a laugh: 'Oh, yeah, I had to change my own studs.' There were shortcomings in their training that I tried to rectify.

In place of Rinus Michels and Ştefan Kovács, the trainer I was dealing with at Ajax was Kurt Linder. He's someone I've learned a lot from. When I showed up at the De Meer Stadion as a player again after signing a new contract in December 1981, the first thing he said was: 'At your age you never have to train too hard. Take special care that your engine never stops.'

So during training I didn't have to run as far or fast as the young guys, because, according to Linder, there was no point. He also kept on checking that I wasn't about to be injured. Linder left after a year, and in my second season I was dealing with Aad de Mos. He was still young for a manager, we were born the same year, and he wanted to learn from me.

When someone wants to do that, you know without knowing it. He asks certain things, he says certain things and then you just talk. So it's not as if you're thinking: Hey, I've got to teach him this or that. No, topics just come up and you talk about them. It was never a problem between us if I knew something he didn't.

So, things were going well for me both on the pitch and in the changing room. I've already said I wasn't happy with the way things were in the boardroom. Thanks to my time with the Washington Diplomats, with a super-manager like Andy Dolich, I was able to recognize a lot of areas with room for improvement. My dissatisfaction would escalate, particularly after the second season.

But first let's go back to the beginning. By returning to the Netherlands I'd found myself back in a land of 70 per cent tax. I got a salary that was the maximum wage in Dutch professional football. Ajax couldn't pay me more than that. However, during negotiations, my advisors had told me that the club could help me to build up a pension fund quite separate from my salary.

Cor came up with a beautiful plan, based on the fact that my presence in the team would increase attendances. Suppose Ajax usually got a crowd of, say, 10,000 for a particular match. We proposed that the gate receipts above that 10,000 figure would be shared between the club and me. If 20,000 turned up, Ajax would benefit by the price of 5,000 tickets and the income from the other 5,000 would go into my pension plan.

We won the championship that first year, drawing huge crowds and earning me a huge amount of money. I couldn't spend it, of course, that was for later on, but the pension plan was an enormous success. And equally so in the second year, not least because a lot of Ajax's matches were played in the Olympic Stadium, which held over 50,000 people. Almost twice as many as De Meer.

At any rate we were busy performing well and at the same time entertaining the public. When things are going well, sometimes you happen on an original idea. Like two players taking a penalty. I did that with Jesper Olsen in the game between Ajax and Helmond Sport. The difference in quality between the two sides was so great that there was no tension in the match. So when we were awarded a penalty we tried to give the fans a bit extra. Rather than shooting I passed it across to Olsen. At first the goalkeeper was perplexed, but when he decided to head towards Jesper, Jesper played the ball back to me. Because I'd stayed in behind the ball, I was onside, and easily able to tap it into the empty goal. People thought it was great.

That season was very positive in every respect but one: the board decided that I was earning too much money. 'But aren't you earning just as much as I am?' I asked. 'Why are you complaining about me, while you are stuffing your own pockets with money? You've never had so many spectators.' They didn't agree with me, so there was a row.

In the meantime, my father-in-law had made good contacts at Feyenoord. When they heard about my problems with Ajax, they immediately said: 'Come to us and we'll set up the same system.' That was very interesting, of course, because at Feyenoord they had a stadium that could hold 47,000 people.

So, in the end, that's what I did. At the end of the 1982–83 season, I signed for Feyenoord. Ajax was still my club, but the people running it refused to go along with me. I heard that they were saying I was too old and too fat, and that I was still putting on weight. I had to deal with all their objections. And they also demanded that I should be satisfied with a normal salary, and of course I wasn't.

I have to say, I had a great time at Feyenoord. Really brilliant. Ajax and Feyenoord are big rivals, so at first I was the bad guy. I had to convince the supporters of my loyalty and make sure that we won. Just as I had done at Barcelona, the Los Angeles Aztecs, the Washington Diplomats and Ajax, I managed to win them over during the first match. I scored a great goal in what was then the Rotterdam Tournament. Everyone started cheering. Then they suddenly seemed to realize that they were cheering for someone they hated. For a moment the whole stadium was in a state of total confusion, but the ice was broken when the supporters saw how happy my teammates were. To round everything off nicely, we went on to win the tournament.

It's often suggested that during my last three years as a player the coaches were only there for show because I called all the shots. That's nonsense. It's not how it works in top-level sport. I'll always remember Kurt Linder as the man who made sure my engine kept running. Aad de Mos was a new name to me, but things worked with him as well. The approach taken by Thijs Libregts at Feyenoord was actually the same as Linder's. When we were cross-country running he always said to me it wasn't important where I finished: 'Run with the rest of them and see how long it takes you.'

As regards the technical and tactical side of things, you mustn't forget that Rinus Michels gave me responsibility to dictate play during the match when I was still very young. At eighteen I already knew automatically when to send someone forward or back on the pitch, or when and how to act for the good of the team. By the time of the 1974 World Cup, of course, I was doing it quite naturally, without thinking about it. So it was never a matter of, 'I'm going my own way here.' That wasn't how it worked. Certainly not when you're partly responsible for the team's tactics during the match. Equally, it was never the case that Linder, de Mos or Libregts did the training while I just played football. It was always a joint effort. It couldn't be the case that I made up for a bad manager, or that a good manager made up for my deficiencies. That's impossible. In the almost three seasons I played after returning to Holland I won three league championships and two KNVB Cups. That only happens when there is sound collaboration between top-level professionals.

It's all about good communication. The manager would give his instructions from the touchline and I would make sure they were carried out on the pitch. That's perfectly normal, of course, not least because there are no time-outs in football. A trainer can give a team talk before the game and during the half-time break, but try to get a message to a player on the opposite wing during the match when fifty thousand people are singing . . . you can't do that. That's when you've got to have someone on the pitch to keep an eye on the big picture.

That's why I often took the throw-in when the ball went out of play near the trainer. Then he could quickly say to me, 'Keep your eye on this, keep your eye on that.' Or else I would ask him something. Not because I thought I was better than anyone else, but as part of a professional way of thinking. For both the trainer and his extension on the pitch, respect has always been crucial. That's why I've never had a row with a trainer. Or almost never. Hennes Weisweiler was the only exception to that rule, when he was trainer with Barcelona for a year. There have never been problems with anyone else.

My last year as an active footballer with Feyenoord was one big party. I did great work with Libregts, and with guys like Ruud Gullit and André Hoekstra we had a great group of players. Joop Hiele, Ben Wijnstekers, Stanley Brard and all the others, everyone was in great form that year. For myself, I'd started the season with the intention of showing my new club something a bit special. That's what happened, and not just a bit. When I think back, I still can't quite grasp it. How in God's name was it possible? Particularly when you think that we'd begun by losing 8–2 against Ajax at the Olympic Stadium, and of all the mockery we got for that. But people forget that something like that is often the start of a resurrection. That's just how it is.

After that 8–2 we won everything. Really everything. The cup, the league and, for me, the Golden Boot for the best footballer in the Eredivisie. By around Easter,

Feyenoord already wanted to extend my contract. But first we played a double bill, with matches on Saturday and Monday, I think. After the second match I felt terrible the next morning. I stumbled downstairs and couldn't actually get back upstairs again. I told Danny: 'I can't keep this up. We've got to call it a day. It's over.' If those two disastrous farewell matches in 1978 were strong indications that my departure from the game wasn't going to go entirely to plan, five years later the fairy-tale ended the way it should. At the top. With football and moments that the people at Ajax and Feyenoord still talk about. Prizes were won too. In three years, three national titles and two cups, which is as good as it gets. So it was OK to end this way. It had been lovely.

I'd like to clear up one misunderstanding. I have never been driven by rancour. Not even in 1983, when I wanted to take my anger out on Ajax via Feyenoord after the club had thrown me out with the rubbish. This so-called revenge that I was supposed to be out for had little to do with my wounded ego, as people often suggest. These things are never as simple as that where I'm concerned.

In 1983 my stepfather, Uncle Henk, had passed away, and that loss affected me so badly that my form at Ajax suffered. The board knew, but the world was told all kinds of implausible stories about me and I was delivered to Feyenoord in a highly damaged state. After that I gathered all my resources to end my career in the spirit of my second father. That gave me the incredible strength to win everything there was to win at the age of thirty-seven. The Eredivisie, the cup, the Golden Boot. The strength his death unleashed in me surprises me still.

After I'd finished with Feyenoord in 1984, I decided to

watch from the sidelines for a year. Observing the game from a distance was very refreshing. It also became clear to me why the Dutch team had failed to qualify for either the 1984 European Championships or the 1982 and 1986 World Cups. The quality of the coaches and the youth academies were under serious discussion. During my sabbatical I saw that there was a terrible shortage of expertise at the clubs. People able to improve the technical qualities of a professional footballer that bit further, aiming straight for the top. There were plenty of characters coming out with all kinds of generalizations, but not so many people who knew how certain aspects ought to be approached.

When I started playing, Jany van der Veen was the youth coach at Ajax. He had been a good player himself, and coached on the basis of the practical experience he'd picked up from his own trainers. During training, he passed on a mixture of his own insights and what he had learned from other people to the new generation of footballers. I remember that those of us on the youth team had to train in the hall when the weather was bad. That wasn't necessarily brilliant. I thought it was pretty useless, in fact. Then van der Veen showed up with some heading games. What else could you do in the hall? He hung up a net that we had to head the ball over, with a team on each side of the net. That way a virtue was made out of a necessity.

Later, I headed in the deciding second goal against Inter in the 1972 European Cup final. It was executed with technical perfection, even though someone of my height shouldn't have been tall enough to make the header. All thanks to a rainy-day exercise that my youth team coach had come up with on the spot. Then came a big shake-up at the KNVB. Now you needed a diploma to be a trainer. But which footballers went and studied for it? Not the street footballers that we were used to. Eventually it became necessary to spend four years studying to become a coach, and now they were an entirely different breed.

Let me take myself as a model. I couldn't have played football and studied at the same time. When I was free the schools were shut, and the schools didn't want to make any exceptions. Via my Cruyff Institute I later tried to give sportsmen a solution, but at the time that's not how people were thinking at all. If you wanted to study as a sportsman, you hadn't a chance. This situation meant that only less-gifted players became trainers. No great footballers went on to study because they'd never find the time. One was the consequence of the other. The ones who weren't stars at their clubs or in the Dutch team didn't have to train every day, so they could go to school. The logical consequence was that the quality of trainers went down, so the quality of football went down. Even though the KNVB now has a shorter period of training for ex-internationals, there's still talk of theoretical training rather than practical train-ing. Little has changed in thirty years. What was once the strength of Dutch football, technical skill, is now our weakness.

In early 1985 my career in football coaching got going in a part-time way when I was taken on as an advisor with Roda JC Kerkrade. Then Leon Melchior asked me to help set up the youth training at MVV in Maastricht. Melchior was an international businessman who had set up a world-renowned racing stables with a lot of top-ranking horses in his free time. MVV had asked his advice in reorganizing the club, and he in turn had sounded me out about helping organize the youth team.

These were the first signs that I was open to a return to football. Shortly after that both Feyenoord and Ajax were knocking at my door. I was particularly pleased that Ajax were showing an interest. It seemed that the club wanted to draw a line under the past. Because I had taken my sporting revenge to the full, I was happy to bury the hatchet.

After that, things speeded up, and in June Ajax appointed me their technical director. It was a newly created post, the first time in the history of Dutch football that the term technical director had been used. It was simply a legal trick that meant I could coach without a coaching diploma. I was originally going to be called head coach, but the trainers' association had threatened to sue the club. 'Technical director' was the term that let Ajax and me move forward.

This might sound a little underhand, but in fact it could be argued that our attitude was supported by the Dutch football association. Early in 1985, I had written a letter to the KNVB asking what I needed to do to be effective as a coach in professional football. I wrote the letter jointly with Rinus Michels, who was by then the association's technical advisor. We were hoping to get the rules changed in such a way that people who actually meant something to professional football because of their knowhow and experience got the chance to make their presence felt.

Because I'd also gained the insight that in real life only the sun rises for nothing, I came up with an alternative to the existing diploma. I suggested that ex-professionals and former internationals should first sit an exam, and then receive tuition in the subjects they'd failed. That way the pace of the course could be easily speeded up, no one would be learning things they knew already and good people would get to the spot where they belonged more quickly. Where they were really needed.

During that period Dutch football was crying out for people who could analyse and improve both a team and eleven individual players. By then I was already of the opinion that the pinnacle could only be reached if you worked away at tiny aspects of play during training. The 1 or 2 per cent. With my idea of first doing the exam and then tailoring the course for the person in question, I was trying to come up with an appropriate solution for the KNVB by quickly attracting more real experts. In doing this, I was taking a big personal risk. In practical terms, I would have breezed through subjects like tactics and technique, but because I thought in such a different way about football from most people, and certainly in a different way from the people running the course, I'd probably never have made it through the exam.

Months went by and I never heard a word from the KNVB. The association had claimed they were going to discuss the matter, but it stopped there. Because it went on so long, in the end we gave up and instead invented the term technical director so that I could get to work at Ajax. Otherwise, I'd have had to become a plaything of the regulations, and I wasn't prepared to do that. Luckily, thanks to my experiences in American soccer, I'd acquired sound insights into how things worked in professional sport, and I could apply my experience to the situation at Ajax. That was vital. The first step was to assume responsibility over the complete footballing environment. From the professionals to the trainees. In this kind of leadership structure, I had to form a team with all the footballing staff. They were the people who had to enforce the policy.

I quickly realized that my role at Ajax didn't sit well with the KNVB or the trainers' association. They came to spy on me and alleged that I was actively taking part in the training sessions. I was easily able to refute that one. I'm not the kind of person who sets people working from his ivory tower. Football's my subject, so I'm at home on the pitch. I used the excuse that because of my hard career as a footballer I needed to work off the pounds, and that was why I was always running around among the players.

But to be perfectly honest, I didn't really ever lead a training session, or barely. I had my technical staff, in the form of Cor van der Hart, Spitz Kohn and Tonny Bruins Slot – three very experienced trainers who compensated extremely well for my lack of experience. Among the players, I was able to work perfectly on the finer details. That's something you don't learn even after a hundred years of training. You have it or you don't. The whole organization of the first team was based on the American model. That meant using specialists. I'd already realized that no single person can be the best footballer in every position on the pitch. That's what I told my technical staff as well.

Apart from the three trainers, Ajax also had a fitness coach. I also took on the first goalkeeping trainer in Holland, who took all the keepers in the club under his wing, from the youth squad to the first team. Later I worked with internal and external scouts as well. I delegated the training sessions, the scouting and so on to others, simply because they were better at it than I was. I've never pretended I could do anything I couldn't. I'd grown up with one trainer and one or two assistants, but during my time I was also influenced by the flower-power movement of the 1960s. By thinking differently. For example, one day at Ajax

I suggested we use Len del Ferro, an opera singer who specialized in breathing techniques, to help the players get the maximum return on every inhalation and exhalation. That's very important in top-level sport. So del Ferro got to work with the players in the changing room. Later, at Barcelona, I brought in a reflexologist, because all the energy in the body always comes out through the feet. You took on someone like that because he might be able to add something new.

So I was always on the lookout for specialists so we could do better work on the details. That was a really important part of my method. In the Netherlands, at least at the beginning of my time in charge at Ajax, they weren't used to working like that. But I said to them: 'If you do fitness training, you're responsible. Not me. So don't ask me what to do. For me, two things are important: in principle they've got to be able to play for 120 minutes, and they have to have a laugh. I'm not the policeman, I'm nothing. But if you can't work it out for yourselves, then I'll go out and find someone else who can.'

So it was about finding people who were both willing to and good enough to take responsibility for their actions. They should never have to think: what would Cruyff think? So the first time each specialist trained the players I usually didn't go along to watch. It was their business and their responsibility.

Most clubs have a main trainer with an assistant, but Ajax suddenly had a technical staff of seven. All the specialist training was based on technique. And by that I don't mean only on-the-ball footballing technique. Take fitness training. It's not about getting a player to the stage where he can run ten kilometres in one go, but making him able to run better because he has better technique. And maybe better running technique helps him to avoid injuries or tiredness during a game. Or makes him faster than his opponent over a short distance.

Running is a whole package that has nothing to do with the ball, but training for it still falls under the heading of 'technique'. In whatever form. The same can apply to other physical aspects of the game. For example jumping and heading. You can propel a ball with your head, but can you really follow through on that with power and direction? There's a huge amount of detail involved in every single aspect of the training.

I did a lot of the footballing detail myself. How is your right arm positioned when you're shooting to the left? How do you get the best balance? What problems are you having and how can you solve them? Or I'd call a meeting with the other specialists to see whether a technical training session could also be used to monitor fitness. Often it's not just a matter of what you want to improve, but also the intensity with which you're training. The result at Ajax was that everyone learned not only how to give the best of themselves, but also how to share it with other people.

I was aware that Dutch football was drifting further and further away from the way we'd surprised the world in 1974. When I went to Ajax I decided from the start to play according to the fundamental principles of Total Football. So goalkeeper Stanley Menzo became a keeper who was also emphatically an outfield player, and one who could be active a long way out of his goal area. This seemed new at the time, but thirty years on it has become commonplace. At places like Barcelona and Bayern it's even rooted in the philosophy of the club. I love seeing that. My intention was to give the Ajax school an identity of its own again. The core principle was to play as much offensive football as possible. We had three strikers and a free man behind them, which meant that opposition defenders had to learn the hard way when they had to mark men or positions.

At that time all teams in the Eredivisie played with two strikers, so I felt I only needed three defenders rather than four. That meant I could play four men in midfield. To do that I usually switched one of the centre backs for the player who is now known as number 10, the shadow striker. By having Menzo no further back than the eighteen-yard line when we had the ball, the rest of the team was pushed far upfield. By choosing Menzo I was also showing how I thought about the composition of a team. I didn't always think of the eleven best footballers, but about a group of players who best fit together. Thus I primarily chose defenders who were the best fit for Stanley. I've always loved puzzling out whether player A is a good fit for player B.

Just as our matches were always entertaining to watch, they also provoked a lot of discussion, which in my view is what professional football ought to do. Some people thought that kind of football was great, while others thought that it would never produce real success. I told everyone that we were bound to be defeated occasionally, but that in the context of our development that was actually unimportant. We were busy investing in the first eleven. The team was already good enough to end up in the top three, however we played, but I wanted more, and to achieve it in a more entertaining way.

As a manager, I stuck to that idea very consistently. Even when we lost a few times I never had doubts about it. Not even later with Barcelona. And every year I won a trophy. During the first season at Ajax it was the KNVB Cup, which earned us a place in the European Cup Winners' Cup. We would win that too in 1987 by beating Lokomotive Leipzig 1–0 in the final in Athens, thanks to a header from Marco van Basten. That Ajax team was the youngest ever to have won a major international competition. Very special, not least because people had been banging on for years about how Dutch clubs hadn't a prayer against the big business interests that ruled in Italy and Spain.

There was another advantage to winning the Cup Winners' Cup. In the end it got a very positive reaction from the KNVB.

About six months after I'd written to the association early in 1985, attempting to set up a shortened training course, I learned that my idea had been turned down. Ajax chairman Ton Harmsen, who was also on the board of the association, told me himself that Michels had voted against it. That seemed very strange, since Michels had both helped me write the letter and presented it to the board in his capacity as technical advisor. This was so that my application would be sent to the right people, but according to Harmsen, Michels did exactly the opposite in the end. I still can't believe it. I never asked Michels about it, because I couldn't imagine it was true. Even today.

Anyway, after Ajax won the European Cup Winners' Cup, the KNVB suddenly dropped all objections to my technical directorship. On 1 June 1987 I wasn't just honoured by the football association for the international success of Ajax, the KNVB also gave me the 'professional football coach' diploma. Of course, that was a one-off gesture. But if I'd been asked to take even a specially shortened course, I'm not sure that I would have done. Both at Ajax and later at Barcelona I never did things that I wasn't in personal control of. For my technical staff I always looked for specialists who complemented me. But then I was lucky to work for two big clubs who could afford to be business-like.

6

Even after I retired from playing I was still more of a hands-on coach than a detached manager, and more of a player than a coach. What I liked best was just playing football with the team. Then we could go on to puzzle about positioning and match strategy. I loved that. Of course, as a coach I was influenced by other people. After all, I've had lots of trainers and coaches. When you've worked with people like Jany van der Veen, Rinus Michels, Georg Kessler, Ştefan Kovács, František Fadrhonc, Hennes Weisweiler, Gordon Bradley, Kurt Linder, Aad de Mos and Thijs Libregts, some of it's going to stick. You take their good points on board and try to learn from their bad ones.

I was partly shaped by all that, although in the end you shape yourself. But by now you might have guessed that van der Veen and Michels have influenced me the most. Van der Veen as a trainer; teaching players how to be technically good. Michels as coach and manager. He was tough as nails, and when you deal with someone like that it leaves its mark. That was already apparent when I did my first bit of coaching, five years earlier than I officially started. While I was still playing with the Washington Diplomats in late 1980, Ajax asked me to become their technical advisor at the end of the American season. Leo Beenhakker was the trainer, and the first eleven wasn't playing at its best. At my first match, in Enschede against FC Twente, I decided to go and sit not in the dugout, but in the stands, because I had the best overview of the pitch from there.

At one point Ajax were 2–3 down, and I saw a few possible ways to turn the match around. I came down from the stands, gave instructions to the players from the sidelines and went to sit next to Beenhakker on the bench. In the end Ajax won 5–3. After the match there was a lot of noise in the press about how I'd made Leo look a fool. But quite honestly I think I'd do exactly the same thing again. Beenhakker knew what I'd been asked to do, and as an advisor you do what the situation calls for. That was the case against FC Twente. Ajax were in danger of losing the match, and I saw the solution to the problem. Then you go and advise, you help out. Which is fine, so long as it works. If it doesn't, everyone is soon after your blood. Fortunately, it all came good. By making a few positional changes, the team became a lot stronger. As a manager, I'd be happy to have an advisor like that. And it's also a snapshot, because immediately after that game it was on to the next match. So I never made a big deal of it. However, that game between Ajax and FC Twente made it very clear where my strength lay. I have total overview not just as a player, but as a coach as well.

Five years later I opted for coaching once and for all. Because I've always liked playing football more than anything else, becoming a coach had always been my second choice. But when I retired from playing I still wanted to be involved in the game. But even then, for me, training has only ever been a substitute for playing. That was why, first with Ajax and later with Barcelona, I tried to ensure that matches were always played as often as possible during pre-season training.

This is an approach that differs from what some other trainers on the continent do during the months of July and August. It's an example of how trainers can differ from one another. Over the years I've noticed they fall into two camps: those who always wanted to be coaches and those who took up coaching because they were no longer fit enough to play. It's clear that I belong to the latter group. And I'm also the kind of trainer who would rather coach and let someone else do the more physical training.

If, as a club executive, you choose someone like me, you'd also have to seriously consider a combination with a 'real' trainer. Someone like Tonny Bruins Slot at Ajax and later at Barcelona complemented me perfectly, for example. He watched the players very closely and was able to keep the training fresh and interesting to help motivate them.

At Ajax, the combination between the then director and vice-chairman Arie van Eijden and me wasn't a happy one. If the board had been aware of how things were, they would never have let us work together. At least not in the way we did. Directors should act as a conduit between the trainer and the board. Someone who's part of the team, just as everyone should be part of the team. From the tea lady to the chairman. In a top club that's how you need to work. Except that wasn't the way they thought at Ajax. Having learned in America how a modern professional club worked, I found myself confronted with an organization that was way behind the times.

I'm sad to say that not much has changed thirty years later. There's a lot more money involved in top-level football, but many of the same mistakes are being made. Consequently, decisions are being made by board members who haven't a clue how best to make them. Choices are made on the basis of personal conversations and lobbying in boardrooms and directors' offices. Sometimes with appalling results, often leaving the trainers involved catching bullets while the decision-makers stay out of the firing line. I'd also like to say that to be a successful trainer requires amazing man-management skills to put the right person in the right place. That's why I'm always amazed when I see someone who isn't the manager making decisions about transfer policy. The fallout from the damage they do can last for years. Millions are wasted, and both trainers and players suffer unnecessarily.

I've experienced that personally as a coach, at both Ajax and Barcelona. In both cases things started well, with the players and me in the spotlight and the board staying in the background. It didn't last: they tried to intervene in playing matters, and in the end got in each other's way. They themselves caused the problems that they later blamed me for. In fact there was tension at Ajax from day one. My experiences in America had taught me a lot about the effect financial differences have on the players. For example, I'd learned from Andy Dolich, the general manager of the Washington Diplomats, how those differences can influence relationships in the changing room and, in an extension of that, results on the pitch.

For that reason I've always paid a lot of attention to the salaries and bonuses received by all my players. For myself, I wasn't even slightly interested, but in training and developing my teams I was forced to follow a particular pattern of thought. For example, you couldn't have player number nine in the pecking order earning more than player number three, simply because one has a smarter agent than the other. Even when salaries are supposed to be confidential, things like that always come out, and make for tension and friction in the dressing room. That was why I wanted to know precisely how much each player earned, to avoid that sort of unrest.

Ajax had also created another problem. In keeping with their financial policy, the club set an upper limit to the transfer fee it would demand when selling any player. That looked all well and good, certainly in the short term, but then the problems started when AC Milan were taken over by the Italian billionaire Silvio Berlusconi in 1987 and the transfer market soared with the input of large amounts of money. With its policy of limited transfer fees, Ajax wouldn't profit from that, but our major competitor PSV Eindhoven would. They got ten times as much from AC Milan for Ruud Gullit as Ajax got for Marco van Basten. There was also the fact that hardly any Dutch clubs shared Ajax's vision. While our best player was walking out the door for a small amount of money, we had to pay the same amount for a replacement from the Eredivisie. At such moments my mouth was my biggest problem. I told the board right out what I thought of them, and held them responsible for undermining the team. It didn't make me any friends.

So, having won the European Cup Winners' Cup in 1987, I found myself in an incredible situation. We had so many possibilities for growing with Ajax, but the management were stifling them. Various times I suggested that van Eijden should do some training with Andy Dolich. It would be good for him and good for Ajax. But the board didn't take me seriously, and didn't do anything about it.

After that the transfer market went completely cock-eyed. Van Basten had gone to AC Milan at a bargain rate and for months I'd had my eye on Coventry City's Cyrille Regis, a physically strong striker with charisma, who was still at the top of his game. Coventry were on a good FA Cup run, and we wanted to act quickly in case his fee soared. A month went by and Ajax hadn't even started seriously negotiating. Coventry won the FA Cup with Regis as the star, and we couldn't afford him any more.

More transfers would fail during that summer of 1987 because the club always waited too long. In the end one of my players, Arnold Mühren, tipped me off that the Irishman Frank Stapleton was available for transfer. They'd played together at Manchester United, and I remembered Stapleton as a great attacker. He didn't cost anything, because he was still vulnerable to injury. That was how I had to get my players in the end.

Our failure to sign Rabah Madjer was the last straw. He'd just won the European Cup with FC Porto, scoring against Bayern Munich with a beautiful backheel shot in a game the Portuguese side won 2–1, and he was a player who really spoke to me. I'd discovered that he was also a huge fan of mine, and dreamed of playing under me. Not only that, but there was a clause in his contract limiting his transfer fee to $800,000. Because of previous transfer failures, I conducted the first part of the negotiations myself. Perhaps I didn't do it very well, but I had no confidence in anyone else. It was only when we'd finished the verbal discussions that I brought in the board and the director. There was a verbal agreement that the transfer absolutely mustn't be leaked before the Ajax–FC Porto UEFA Super Cup match, which was due to be played a week later. The Portuguese were very firm on that. The Super Cup was first prize as far as they were concerned, and they didn't want to give the impression that they were willing to blow it by making this transfer.

The terms were quite clear, and the transfer shouldn't have gone wrong. But it did, in a way that made it quite clear how bad things had become at Ajax. Only two board members and the director had been fully briefed on the agreement with Porto, and one of them would leak the story to the press the day before the match, after which a furious Porto chairman informed me that the transfer deal was off the table. Then Bayern picked up Madjer, and I had been overtaken by events again.

I was moving from one problem to another. At Ajax, van Basten had always been the undisputed star. After he moved to AC Milan I was forced to make up for not only his quality but also his authority. Because I wasn't getting the players I wanted, I had to make a choice from the existing team. After van Basten left, I wanted to find another natural leader in the group. Frank Rijkaard was the name that came to mind. He was our best player, yes, but for all kinds of reasons it wasn't working out. Frank is modest by nature, and I tried to change that. Unfortunately his discontent escalated, and he gave up playing for Ajax almost overnight. He suddenly wasn't interested any more; he was fed up with it all. I was completely shocked. But I'd also like to make it clear that this problem wouldn't have occurred if the club's management had operated professionally in the transfer market.

Unfortunately, my message to Rijkaard that I was just trying to help him as a footballer fell on deaf ears. I find it impossible to improve somebody who doesn't want to learn. I can't put my energy into it. Certainly, in top-level sport you have to be tough about people's failings, and make it quite clear what needs to be done to eradicate them.

That also applies to the players who were still failing to show progress at the end of the season. Again and again I was forced to learn how tough I had to be on myself. But because you have to keep on choosing your best team, you're almost obliged to forget the person who's wearing the shirt. The most difficult thing in the world, but you have no choice. As soon as you start making allowances for one player, there'll be another one who won't cooperate, and in the end the whole group of players will slip through your fingers.

That's how it works at the top, and quite honestly I can't think any other way to approach it. It's probably my shortcoming. I can't put myself in the position of someone who won't do what I'm asking them to. A player has to be able to learn something from me. Because if he doesn't learn, then it's goodbye. I have to keep moving forward. Annoyingly, the worst offenders are often the nicest people. Yet they're the ones you've got to get rid of. That always felt very frustrating, not least because in some cases they'd even become friends. The break with Rijkaard, however, was of a different order. Bad business management had affected the balance within the team, and I was forced too soon to push him into a leadership role he wasn't ready for.

As a coach I've always wanted a team with a good mix of players I've trained myself, some young scouted talent, and a few new purchases bought to strengthen the team. At Ajax we were doing fantastically well in that respect. The supporters enjoyed our play, and we had given Aron Winter and, at the age of seventeen, Dennis Bergkamp their debuts.

I'd also persuaded a few big Amsterdam businessmen to put a million guilders into Ajax youth training. That was an incredibly large sum for the time. Certainly where developing talent is concerned.

Although the stadium was full and Ajax was winning trophies again, the board was becoming increasingly intrusive. That had become apparent during the 1987 summer transfer period, but even after that they wanted to intervene more and more in the technical side of things. By early 1988 I'd had enough. While I was taking a skiing holiday the chairman, Ton Harmsen, told me on the phone that he'd solved my problems with the club management. I just had to talk to the whole board and everything would sort itself out. I came back early from holiday, but it seemed as though Harmsen had been pulling my leg. Rather than being conciliatory, the other board members went into full attack mode. Harmsen just sat there and watched.

I'd reached my limit, and the next day I resigned. However much I'd wanted to stay in Holland, however pleased I'd been to be back with Ajax, I couldn't stay. I must admit, I had a few sleepless nights over it, because my family were having such a good time in Amsterdam. But there was nothing to be done. Ajax wanted to finish me off, and unfortunately a few journalists went along with it. I felt that they wanted to destroy everything I'd built. I didn't let them do that. I wanted to go down sticking to my guns. After that they ran out of steam. You can't go around damaging people. The board did that first when I was a player and later again as a coach. You can't do that and expect to get away with it. And nothing good ever happened between us ever again.

Everything had felt so good at Ajax and suddenly it was

over. It was a very strange time for me. I'd won a European Cup Winner's Cup when no one expected it. And I'd been forced to leave because I'd wanted to take the club to a higher level. By now, the facts spoke for themselves. Three times I'd come to Ajax and the trophy cabinet had been empty. Now I was leaving for the third time, and again the cabinet was full.

Luckily, I have many more good memories than bad from my time there. That's thanks especially to the players. Both as a player and as a trainer I was working with a fantastic group. All really great people. The fun we had seemed in the end to have been how we stuck together for so long. Until it all became impossible and I even found myself rowing with someone like Frank Rijkaard. Luckily, Frank and I sorted things out later, but it was shocking that it had even come to that.

My family's desire to settle in Holland once and for all was sadly unfulfilled. Again I was being forced out of Ajax, and again my destination was Barcelona.

I said before that I play football most of all to entertain the public. For me it isn't just a question of winning. My principles have always been built on the questions: how well are you going to win? And what approach are you going to take to do it? And you always have to take the fans into account. The supporters who are sitting in the stands, the ones for whom the club is part of their lives. As a player or a coach you have to put yourself in those people's heads a lot. In Holland they think differently from the way they do in Germany, or in England, or in Spain or Italy. Their characters are different. That's why you can't play like an Italian if you live in Holland. You just can't. Whoever you are and wherever you come from.

One of the great advantages I had as a trainer of Barcelona was that I'd played there too. I knew the way of thinking there, and I knew how the limits of that thinking could change to provide a certain quality. To be able to do that you have to be aware of the Catalan way of life, the politics, the national character. At Barcelona I first had to come to terms with a tradition. The one of having a big name, a lot of money and no silverware. So in that respect they were at a slightly lower level than Ajax. Also, every player in Amsterdam thought about attacking, while everyone in Barcelona played backwards. So I had to start by changing their pattern of thought.

And that's important to me too. I only want to work for clubs who want to play football. To play football the way it should be played. Technically good, and attractive. I want to feel the atmosphere; smell the changing room. A club that plays in a stadium with an athletic track is of no interest to me. The pitch and the changing room should never be far from each other. Players must have the feeling that they can step on to the pitch from their own familiar surroundings. It's great too, and a big advantage, if young players can train as they can at Ajax or Barcelona, where they can see the stadium in the background. The place they hope to play one day.

For me football is an emotion. As a player I couldn't even imagine spending my time stifling others' play, and I didn't want to get bored sitting on the bench, so I was always looking for ways to improve. As a trainer I want to enjoy myself, and strive for perfect football. Then the results happen all by themselves. Wherever I've worked, I wanted the people I've worked with to speak and think about football. All day, if possible. At Barcelona that all-embracing football atmosphere was missing. No one had a story. That was the main thing I wanted to give to the club and the fans. To get them talking about football, talking about how it should be played. Even the gossip should be about football.

Setting that in motion is a matter of using your own free spirit and having a lot of resilience. I see this kind of thing as a jigsaw puzzle of problems. I see one problem and I immediately try to solve it, though in a way that will make it easier to place the next piece in the puzzle. In the end it pays off. It's a game that you're dealing with, after all. A really nice game.

Of course, I was made even more wary of club politics by what had happened to me as a trainer at Ajax, but to my mind the situation at Barcelona was possibly even worse than it had been in Amsterdam. There were constant crises all over the place, one row after the other. La Liga had been won only once in the past dozen years and by now attendances had dwindled to barely 40,000, when once they were more than double that. So I knew why the club president Josep Lluís Núñez was so keen to have me. He was mostly busy saving his own position. He had been President from 1978, the year I had left the club as a player, and now he would be the one to bring me back. I wasn't brought in because he supported my vision but simply in the hope that I would fill the trophy cabinet. I was a political means to an end. I knew that beforehand, but my experience at Ajax had prepared me, and so I set out my requirements in advance.

One demand was that I would be the only boss in the

changing room. So, not the players, not the board, me. If the board wanted to discuss something I would go to them, because I didn't want to see them in the changing room. I made that very clear to Núñez beforehand, knowing that he didn't agree with it. Presidents like him are used to everyone doing what they say, but I turned that on its head. Partly because of that, we never had a warm relationship.

The cards were reshuffled during the preseason presentation. The public started clapping for Núñez and hissing at Alexanco, whom I'd just appointed captain. I grabbed the mic and told the supporters that I might just quit if they kept on like that. The reason was that, during an earlier dispute with the club management, Alexanco had supported his fellow players. He had shown character, and that was exactly the kind of person needed to bring Barcelona back up to the top. So I told the fans I didn't want to have anything to do with the recent past of Barcelona. That past consisted of hatred and envy between everyone inside the club. I wasn't interested in that. I didn't want to work that way and I asked the supporters to back me in that.

After that, I threw everything open to the press. The papers needed to be full of Barça again, but in a good way. I've learned that either you can work with the media or you can work against it. So I said: 'I'm going to help you. You can write, analyse and interpret what you like, but if you talk to us, please write down very accurately what the players and I say.'

Our training sessions were never held behind closed doors. It was good for the atmosphere and the bond with the public was strengthened as a result. Sometimes I could even use it to my advantage if a player had to be put in his place. For example, early on I had this right-footed player who'd got too big for his boots, and I made him shoot at the goal with his left foot. The ball flew off in all directions and the fans were helpless with laughter. The problem was solved at a stroke.

Then I set to work. First by minimizing the small mistakes. As I've said, the problems seldom or never come from the big mistakes, it's often the small ones that count. That's where coaching begins too. That's why I also trained alongside the players. You see more that way, and you can intervene appropriately.

Other times I just sat on a ball by the side of the field and watched. There were people who said I was lazy. That's as may be, but if I'm sitting still I see more than if I move round. Sitting like that, I can analyse someone better, and see the details more clearly. Often details that 99 per cent of people don't know, don't see or don't understand.

From the start, I turned things round at Barcelona. What I found when I got there was a style of play in which defenders had to run less than attackers. I wanted to change that straight away, though always keeping in mind the fact that football is about adding up metres. It's about thinking things through creatively but logically.

And, as I have already said, I like to turn traditional thinking on its head, by telling the striker that he's the first defender, by helping the goalkeeper to understand that he is the first attacker and by explaining to the defenders that they determine the length of the playing area. Based on the understanding that the distances between the banks of players can never be more than ten to fifteen metres. And everyone had to be aware that space had to be created when they got possession, and that without the ball they had to play tighter. You do that effectively by keeping your eye on each other. So as soon as one player starts running, the other one tracks him.

Training is a process that players have to be invested in day in, day out. And as soon as it looked that they were starting to get bored, I'd come up with another exercise that made us laugh. For me it was a matter of using space, gauging metres. I did that so much that someone once asked me if I was some sort of maths nerd. (It's possible, I've always been fascinated by numbers and distances.) I tried to translate that as efficiently as possible so the players could understand it. Take the combination of Ronald Koeman, who I signed in 1989, and Pep Guardiola, who I promoted to the first team in 1990, as the central defence duo at Barcelona. They weren't fast, and they weren't defenders. But we always played in the opponent's half. I calculated the odds on the basis of three passes that the opposing team could make. First the ball deep in the field that's played over our last line. If the keeper was good, and positioned a long way away from the goal, it would always be his ball. Then the cross-field pass. I had fast full backs for that, who were trained as wingers. They were always there in time to intercept the ball. The third option was the pass down the centre. Guardiola and Koeman had such positional strength that they always intercepted it, even though they were clearly not the ideal midfielder–defenders. That was probably why it worked. Because the keeper was in a good position and the full backs were used in the right way.

So we were constantly working with defenders to find that kind of solution. Like putting on the pressure not by sprinting thirty metres, but by moving a few metres at the right moment. Then I explained that everyone who you give five metres of space looks like a good footballer, because they are not under any pressure. If you tackle from three metres away, it's another story. To be able to play like that you need to be fast, and you have to keep switching gear. It took more than 10,000 hours of training to finally reach the level of the Dream Team, as the squad of that era is often called.

That's why I like sports that involve a lot of tactics, like baseball and basketball. As a baseball player, in my youth, I learned always to think one step ahead, but in football that's not enough. You need to think further ahead than that. Because there's no time-out in football, training sessions have to cover all eventualities.

Just like at Ajax, success came almost at once. People thought the new style was great, and soon the stadium was filled by crowds of over 90,000. We also had an advantage in that while more and more teams were adopting a defensive style of play, we were mostly busy scoring goals. Everything was in place. Usually it worked, sometimes it didn't, but there was always something entertaining going on. There was a dynamism in our play, and a lot happened in front of the goal.

The starting-point of our free-scoring style was the three-striker system, with two wing players and the intention of pinning down the other side in their own half. That saved a lot of running, which meant everyone was fit to take the initiative. Physically and mentally. That was why we had to train so often and so intensively. The more instinctive our play became, the less mental energy it would require. That way something was created that looked difficult but was actually easy. You're 100 per cent concentrated on the task at hand, but because you automatically knew what to do, you didn't notice.

That 100 per cent concentration is vital if you're going to play positional football, with new triangles forming every time and the player with the ball always having two possible passes. However, it's the third man who determines his choice. With that last point, I want to stress that it isn't the man on the ball who decides where the ball goes, but the players without the ball. Their running actions determine the next pass.

That's why I go crazy when I see players standing still on the pitch. To play like that for me is out of the question. In possession, eleven men have to be in motion. Busy fine-tuning distances. It's not a question of how much you run but where you run to. Constantly creating triangles means that the ball circulation isn't interrupted.

Because we had to start from zero in Barcelona, it took four years before we reached our peak by winning the European Cup in 1992. Until then it was a question of very targeted training, good workouts and shrewd signings. You had to be very sharp about those, because the rule about fielding a maximum of three foreign players was still in force. So that was a very different way of scouting from today, when you can have an unlimited number of foreigners in a squad and in the team. That's why we couldn't grumble about choosing players like Hrist Stoichkov, Michael Laudrup and Ronald Koeman. Stoichkov and Laudrup barely cost Barcelona anything.

Even though we didn't win La Liga in the first year, 1989, we did – just as Ajax had done before – win the European Cup Winners' Cup, beating Genoa's Sampdoria 2–0 with goals from Julio Salinas and López Rekarte. We won the Copa del Rey in the second season as well, and after that it was really time to bring in the harvest. The change in style of play was pretty well complete, so we had to do some work on the improvement of our positions. Not least by bringing in someone like Hristo Stoichkov, a then unknown Bulgarian, who was also – once again – cheap. Hristo was someone I needed not only because of his footballing qualities, but also because of his character. He was a fighter, and obstinate in a good way. In a team in which there weren't actually all that many strong characters, he was the type who could shake things up. Not only in the changing room, but also on the pitch.

During that time I was getting stomach complaints more and more often. Sometimes I would just start sweating, or suddenly throw up. I'd already cut down on my smoking, but in late February 1991 my wife intervened. She urged me to go with her to the hospital, and they kept me in. The veins around my heart seemed to have silted up. In a three-hour operation I was given two bypasses. Luckily I hadn't been having heart attacks. Rather, it was atherosclerosis, a thickening of the arteries.

Being ill didn't make me nervous for a moment. My experience of the whole process was that if so many people were busy making me better, it wouldn't make much sense for me to remain ill afterwards. And at such moments it's a great help to be famous. When your heart surgeon knows damned well that the whole world will be watching, then you know in advance that the man is going to make a point of doing his best during the operation. That was a great feeling.

After that, I became more and more aware that I had been helped and treated in order not to give up on life, but to make the most of it. Since then I've also been freed of all worries about an early death. The idea that I, like my father, would die young is an obsession I've shaken off entirely since my heart problems. Completely.

The main lesson I've learned from it is that you can't do anything that's bad for you and not expect to be punished. Like whether or not you smoke. Since my operation I've gone on living in much the same way I did before. My attitude was: get on with normal life as quickly as possible. But probably with a few new rules. Of course I thought a lot after my illness about my smoking addiction. I wondered why I'd smoked so much for so long. Especially after the doctors had told me that 90 per cent of my heart problem was caused by smoking. Then you start thinking about it. And I realized how incompatibly I'd been living for years. I knew that smoking could cause cancer, I knew it was bad for my heart, and I still kept on fooling myself, using the excuse that it was a good way of fighting stress. I had absolutely no trouble coming up with reasons not to quit.

After the operation I switched completely to the other side. The good side. I gave up smoking overnight. It was banished from my life. At the same time I became enamoured of the idea of giving a clear signal to others. Not like a kind of sandwich man for all kinds of anti-smoking campaigns – and I was inundated with requests to do just that – but by doing something that would suit me completely, something that would be effective. Something that would provoke both action and reaction, something with a universal moral. I wanted anyone, anywhere in the world, to be able to understand it. That's how we came up with the idea of a video clip, financed by the Catalan Health Ministry. In that film I'm keeping in the air not a ball, but a pack of cigarettes. Every time I touch the box with my head, shoulder, knee or foot, you hear a heartbeat. And I say, 'Football has always been my life.' After a short silence I suddenly kick the pack away, and it immediately blows apart. Then I finish with, 'And smoking almost cost me my life.' The clip was overdubbed in Spanish, Catalan, English, French and Dutch and went all the way round the world. That was exactly the kind of message I wanted.

My heart problems led to another discovery. Three weeks after my operation the doctors decided to monitor me around the time of an important Barcelona match, one about which there was a lot of excitement, to investigate how my heart would hold up under severe pressure. This was Barcelona–Dynamo Kiev in the quarter finals of the 1991 European Cup Winners' Cup. A special apparatus was sent from the Sant Jordi hospital, with all kinds of wires and buttons that were stuck to my chest. That way they were able to follow the rhythm of my heart during the match, which I watched at home in front of the telly. Even though it was a hugely exciting game that Barcelona only decided in the last minute, my cardiac rhythm didn't accelerate at all. Later, they also tested it when I was sitting in the dugout, but even then nothing unusual happened. There was even one match in which my heart rhythm remained as steady as someone having an afternoon nap. My heartbeat was only recorded going up once: at a meeting with the Barcelona board.

Exactly a month after my operation I was back as coach, and a few weeks later Barça won the Spanish championship for the first time under my management. I spent the match not lighting cigarettes, but with a lollipop in my mouth. I thought it was delicious and it gave me something to combat the stress which, according to the medical examinations, I didn't even have.

So 1991 was a very special year, and very instructive, because after winning the Spanish title we lost the European Cup Winners' Cup final against Manchester United 2–1. The way we lost in particular, which was much more to do with bad luck than anything else because we played very well, made it clear to me that while we might have taken some big steps, we certainly hadn't reached the final goal.

That didn't happen until the next season. That was another special, beautiful and happy year in every respect. It started with the transfer of Richard Witschge from my old club Ajax to Barcelona. A new board had just been appointed in Amsterdam, with my old friend Michael van Praag as chairman. The previous board, which had fired me, seemed to have left a big financial mess behind, and had saddled the club with millions of debt.

I honestly admit that I got Barcelona to pay a bit more for Witschge to get Ajax out of its difficulties. I think $8 million were transferred, when we could have done it for $6 million. But fine, we'd spent so little on players for years that Barcelona owed me a little bit.

It began an unforgettable year. Not least the month of May 1992. First there was the wedding of my daughter Chantal and a week later Barcelona won the European Cup for the first time.

No shortage of good luck, then. And that included football, too. In the year that we were the best in Europe, we were almost knocked out in the second round by the German champions, FC Kaiserslautern. José María Bakero scored the deciding goal in the very last second; otherwise we would never have made it to the final against Sampdoria. It was a rescue not unlike the goal that Andrés Iniesta scored years later in the last seconds against Chelsea, when Barcelona went on to win the Champions League final against Manchester United.

It goes to show the extent to which luck is often directly connected with success. But then you have to command that luck. That's why I've always taken the initiative as a footballer. Directing the match. To make sure I'm in control of things. As I did on 20 May 1992 at Wembley against Sampdoria. After ninety minutes the score was still 0–0 and Ronald Koeman would score that historic goal in extra time. After four years my mission had been accomplished. That evening the team on the pitch was the one I'd always had in my imagination. A team that spoke to the public, that liberated something in the supporters and was a mixture of self-trained Catalans and cleverly scouted reinforcements. Of course, I had an emotional reaction. The picture of me clambering over an advertising hoarding went all around the world, and is typical of one of those moments when you do something you can't explain, even to yourself. You do it because it's the first thing that occurs to you. Maybe it was emotion, but maybe it wasn't. I had to get out on the pitch, and climbing over it was the quickest way. So maybe I was just using common sense.

The whole of Catalonia went mad after the win in London. Joy was completely unbounded when, a few weeks later, we became league champions for the second time in a row. It was incredible but true. We had been at the top of the league only once that season, and that was after the last round of matches. We won at home against Athletic Bilbao, and Real Madrid lost 3–2 against Tenerife. In emotional terms, that championship was even more powerful than the win at Wembley. We all stood in the centre circle waiting for the final whistle in Tenerife; you never forget something like that.

Sadly, Ronald Koeman didn't get to experience that special feeling. Rinus Michels, who was then coach of the Dutch team, had taken him off for an international practice match. When I heard that, I thought it was some kind of joke. How does a footballer cope with something like that? And from Michels, of all people! I didn't understand it at all. You play for a whole year for the title and then you can't come and pick up the reward; it had got too stupid.

7

It may sound like a contradiction, but in Barcelona's most successful season, 1991–92, the problems were created that would later lead to the break between me and the club. Once again there was a parallel with Ajax, after we had won the European Cup Winners' Cup in 1987. As long as there's success, everyone joins in the day's madness. That was typical of Barcelona too: while the euphoria was still there, contracts were extended, even for players who hadn't performed. So, Núñez and vice-chairman Joan Gaspart took charge of everything again. Gaspart was responsible for the contracts, but, of course, he was an extension of the president. And in spite of our successes I had a purely businesslike relationship with Núñez. I just didn't trust him. He was never able to take away the feeling from me that I was only there to keep him on the throne. I always felt I needed to be strong, or else I would find myself in difficulties.

It was already clear how success had influenced everyone from the start of the new season. In the second round of the 1992–93 Champions League we were knocked out by CSKA Moscow 4–3 on aggregate. That December, we lost the Intercontinental Cup match against São Paulo 2–1. It was one of the few times that I had no problems with a defeat. I've always admired the Brazilian coach Telê Santana for his vision, because it always displayed a genuine love of football. That man had had the honour of managing Brazil in the World Cup of 1982. The defeat of that fantastic team by Italy made me think of our defeat against Germany in 1974. Even more than Italian success, what people remember is the way Brazil played, and the names of that fantastic midfield, with Zico, Sócrates, Falcão and Cerezo.

Ten years later, Telê Santana was coach of the South American champions São Paulo, and he sent a dream team of his own to the match with us in Tokyo. After the game I told the press: if you're going to get run over, it's better if it's a Rolls-Royce that does it.

Again our domestic season would be saved on the last day. And again we were inadvertently helped by Tenerife, who defeated Real Madrid 1–0, allowing us to clinch the title. A year later we got a helping hand for the third year in a row. In 1994 Deportivo de La Coruña were the front-runners, but missed a penalty in the last minute of the last match of the season, leaving their score against Valencia 0–0. Just enough for us to become champions for the fourth time in succession.

We also reached the Champions League final in 1994 against AC Milan, a match that we had to play a few days after celebrating the championship. That was another example of how things can go wrong if you take a step too early or a step too late, but not in time. Then it's an accumulation of little mistakes which can lead to a 4–0 defeat against an excellent opponent.

After that, more and more problems came to the surface. For six years Barcelona had been on the way up. With players who had grown with the club. As with Ajax, the great thing was that we didn't just have a talented team, but also brilliant people. Athletes who gave a lot of positive energy not just to me, but to others as well.

In my private life I had good relations with various young lads in the squad. I've never kept my private life and my work life completely separate. I regularly went out to restaurants with them, or celebrated their birthdays. In professional terms I tried hard to maintain a good relationship too. Of course, players were disappointed if they were passed over. On the other hand I was also a coach who, if one of my squad ended up in hospital, went to the operating theatre to check that the knife wasn't going into the wrong leg. To put injured players at ease, I made a habit of being present at operations, reassuring them that, if the trainer was there, everything would be fine. I had to put on a surgical suit with a little hat and a mask over my mouth. That relaxed the player, and it was my responsibility to do that.

As a result, over the years I became increasingly fascinated by medical science. Most surgeons were perfectly happy with the arrangement, and allowed me to be present at all kinds of operations. One of the most interesting was a brain operation in the hospital that the club doctor of the Washington Diplomats was involved with. It was amazing to see part of the skull being removed, and the problem being solved with incredible precision. I really enjoy watching real experts carrying out specialized procedures.

Over the years I've witnessed dozens of operations, and I've been given a good insight into the subject, particularly where leg surgery is concerned. In the end I was able to foresee how things would go wrong at Barcelona in that respect, because we just didn't have enough of the best people to look after the players.

After six years of building, the turning point came in

the 1994–95 season. This was the phase in which the club had to think hard about how we were going to replace the successful but ageing team, one step at a time. In a process like that it's essential that the club management understands what's happening. That they appreciate what the long-term strategy is, and that everyone is able to stand above the madness of the day. So, for example, Michael Laudrup and our goalkeeper, Andoni Zubizarreta, were to leave for Real Madrid and Valencia, respectively. There was a lot of discussion about it, but I just didn't want to run the risk of great players like that ending up on the bench. They didn't deserve to be the twelfth man.

In situations like that there has to be a common front between trainer and boardroom. That was the time for Núñez to reassure me that I wasn't just there for him, but that we were working together for FC Barcelona. But in fact he only confirmed that the suspicions I'd had about him for all those years were correct. Like Ton Harmsen at Ajax, Núñez started sniffing around the press. And, as had happened in Holland, only a few journalists saw through him.

The single highlight of that season was the first-team debut of my son Jordi. On 10 September 1994 he turned out for the Barcelona against Santander. He was just twenty, and he immediately scored the first goal, an important contribution to the final 2–1 victory. Unfortunately my presence at the club brought him mostly trouble from Núñez.

My last season, 1995–96, could have been a copy of my last months at Ajax. While for years we'd operated quickly and successfully in the transfer market, in 1995 the board suddenly started grumbling about it. So, for example, I wanted to bring the talented Zinedine Zidane in from Bordeaux, but they didn't think much of him and nothing came of it. I also noticed more and more often that my position was being undermined, including by some of the doctors we worked with. Some felt that they were untouchable. The worst was an operation for which a team of specialists was brought in to operate on one of the players. Outside the operating theatre one of the doctors suddenly turned round and said, 'This is my hospital and I'm the only person who operates here . . .' Because the player was already in the theatre, there was nothing anyone could do about it. Even though there were people present who were much more skilled in that particular field than he was, his ego was more important to him than anything else. More important than the welfare of the club and the player.

The sad low point of that, as far as I was concerned, was the operation that Jordi had to undergo at the end of 1995. It involved a meniscus, for an orthopaedic surgeon pretty much the simplest intervention that exists. Unfortunately, the operation didn't go to plan, with appalling consequences for Jordi's career. Even today he still has trouble with his knee. Jordi was slightly bow-legged, and with a patient like that it's a requirement that the surgeon doesn't just perform the operation on the knee, but also has to take into account the balance in the joint; otherwise you end up with a bigger problem. It's very sad, in fact, because after the operation he was never able to train at 100 per cent, which meant that he wasn't able to make the most of his abilities.

It was already clear by April 1996 that, for the first time since my arrival in 1988, we weren't going to win a trophy that season. I wasn't dissatisfied with the steps we'd taken to renew the team, but there were other, negative things which, as representative of all the players, I couldn't accept. More and more information was being withheld, and agreements weren't being honoured. It was a nasty situation, and relationships were getting worse all the time. Then I suddenly read in the paper that I'd been fired and that Núñez and Gaspart were about to introduce Bobby Robson as my successor. An unreal situation. A few days before, I had had a conversation with Núñez about the forthcoming season, and personally persuaded Luis Enrique to move from Real Madrid to Barcelona. The lad did that for *me*. Núñez knew that, but he kept quiet about my imminent sacking.

Perhaps the worst thing was that I was temporarily replaced by my friend and right-hand man Charly Rexach. Particularly because he reacted as if it was the most natural thing in the world. Rexach of all people, who had always been more extreme in his resistance to Núñez than me. During his first training session he immediately got it in the neck for his choices. Jordi actually refused to train under him. It turned straight into a row. In the end a decision was made to pick Jordi for the home game against Celta de Vigo, to make sure that the public didn't go mad. Luckily, that turned into a fantastic memory. After Barça went 2–0 down, Jordi was one of the athletes who ensured the game was won 3–2 in the end. But best of all was the fact that, after the winning goal, he left the pitch and forced Rexach to grant him a standing ovation. Once it was over Jordi explained that he had wanted to give the fans the opportunity to thank his father.

And that also turned out to be Jordi's last match for Barcelona.

Just like with Ajax, it was sad that things had to end like

that at Barcelona. I saw it as a kind of mission of mine to change, at long last, the image Barcelona had gained that, while they might have been the richest club, they never played in the best or most beautiful way. So the fact that I'd been successful didn't just mean I'd achieved a target, it also showed that my commitment had gone beyond that of just being a trainer. But the biggest problem at Barcelona is the club itself. It's all about politics. That also explains my aversion to the circus of executives who use sentiment for their own ends and are only ever driving their clubs into the ground. But in the end they unmask themselves. That happened at Ajax with Harmsen, and later at Barça with Núñez too. I'm glad I'm out of it.

My career has obviously had a big effect on my family. We have a real bond, and we've always tried to let all the madness going on outside influence us as little as possible, but it wasn't easy for Danny, Chantal, Susila and Jordi. Of all my children, Jordi was the most affected, but that pressure also shaped him into the special man he is now. Almost all of my career decisions have reached deep into my son's life. In 1983, when I had to leave as a player with Ajax, he was left behind while I took my revenge on his club via Feyenoord. When I later left De Meer as a trainer, he had to leave his club and his pals behind once again. I went on influencing his life after that as well. Because in Barcelona people kept telling him, as they had done in Amsterdam, that he was only in the team because he was the coach's son.

That was why his debut in the Dutch national squad and later his participation in the 1996 European Championship was the best thing that could have happened to me. His selection by the national manager Guus Hiddink was a self-contained affair; I had absolutely no influence on it whatsoever. My emotion reached its high point during the Euros in Birmingham, when Jordi scored the first goal against Switzerland. At such moments everything flashes through your head. The harassment, the gossip, the misery and then, thirty metres below me on the pitch, the proof that he'd come out of it all unscathed. Your pride knows no bounds. I don't tend to have many emotional moments like that. Sometimes there are goosebumps when someone delivers an extraordinary performance. If someone's merely good, it doesn't mean much to me, but it affects me greatly if he's able to bring that something extra, like the athlete Edwin Moses once did, winning more than a hundred finals in a row. I thought that was so fantastic, incredibly good. Because it's very human to be blasé when you're that good and you win that much. And yet for years he stuck with the attitude of delivering a world-class performance on Wednesday and improving it on Sunday. If you can manage that, you're really great, and more than just a sportsman.

It's a quality that you actually see in all exceptional top-level sportsmen. Those at the very top, whatever sport they're doing, need to win from the moment the referee blows the whistle or the starting gun is fired. It's a culture that certain people have inside them, and it's more than just quality. It's something in your head and in your body, and it comes to the surface at the most beautiful moments of all.

The players who have it are the ones who know both that excellence is difficult, and just how difficult it is. People like me, who have had to summon this same culture from inside, have a deep respect for it. They feel that at any given moment they have something to prove and that they will prove it. That's extremely good. It's a mystery, and it isn't just about talent. It's about fine-tuning every little detail. And, of course, you need quality or else you aren't going to get there. I've always enjoyed watching the very best top-level players.

Hence, too, my pride in Jordi, who has pretty much always done what he had to do. Even when he was a boy I saw that he had a talent for football. In the way he kicked a ball, for example. But in the early years you couldn't say that I paid attention to it every day. We were living in an apartment in Barcelona, and, of course, in a flat like that you're just messing about with the ball. You're busy with a football, but not really busy playing football. That didn't happen until my time with Ajax, when Jordi was about ten. Before that I mostly let him go his own way. Later, in America, he was able to play football in the street, unlike in Barcelona. They also had summer camps there, where children were kept busy playing soccer all day. Washington was a particularly European-oriented city, and lots of the people sent their children to camps like that. It was good for Jordi to be able to improve his English and play some decent sport.

After we moved back to Holland, he was able to train with Ajax. Jordi was suddenly able to play reasonably well. It just got better, because we had a little football pitch at the back of the garden at our house in Vinkeveen. With goals. Then it really got fantastic. Not least because I saw that he was a good player, in an odd way. Jordi was left-footed, but you only saw that when he took penalties. He actually didn't seem so good with his right. That's a curious thing to discover at such a young age.

From boyhood onwards Jordi had to face a particular challenge, and one not unrelated to my own fame. If he played a bad match, he had the qualities of his mother, and if he played a good one, he had the qualities of his father.

You can deal with something like that, but it was a different kettle of fish when I went to play for Feyenoord and he stayed at Ajax. That was a very difficult time. That's why I'm all the more grateful to the squad manager, Henk van Teunenbroek, for immediately making Jordi captain of his junior squad. That was a very special gesture. Certainly for such a young kid. Some things stay with you. His coach turned round what could have been a very damaging situation for Jordi. At that point it was the most important thing anyone could have done for my son. Good thinking on van Teunenbroek's part. That was enormously valuable to me. Incidentally, I can't remember anyone at Ajax ever saying anything nasty to Jordi. Anything about having an advantage or whatever, just because he happened to be my son. I'd probably have heard about it from Danny, who always went along with him while he was a youngster. When I was still playing football, and later coaching at Ajax, that was almost impossible for me.

Even though Ajax was very much to Jordi's liking, in 1988 he was still only fourteen, so he had to come with us to Barcelona. There too he got through trials, and played football there during the eight years that I was coach. Every year he came a step closer to the first team, and at last, in 1994, I thought he was good enough. At the age of twenty he was quite old to be making his debut, but it didn't matter. It wasn't all a bed of roses. As soon as he found himself in Barcelona as a teenager, he had to deal with the curious situation that, as a foreigner, he could play in regional competitions but not national ones. That was crazy. Jordi could be in the B-team, which played in the Catalan competition, but not in the first team, which played at national level.

That's the kind of thing that Dutch people won't put up with. So I engaged in a spot of provocation. I rang the federation and said, 'I'm calling to inform you that he's just going to play for the first team on Sunday. Just so that you know, if you want to suspend people or anything. But I won't accept that. I live here, I'm a Dutchman, I'm Barcelona's trainer, so I'm not just passing through. My son has the same rights as any other kid in Spain or Catalonia or wherever. I'm not going to accept any opposition. I pay my taxes, I do everything that any normal person does, so my kids have the same rights.' Jordi was picked, played the match and there were no recriminations. I think the federation worked out at last that it wasn't on. That they'd overlooked an old rule and forgotten to change it.

But OK, I'm mostly trying to say that there's been a lot going on around Jordi. It's not by chance that people talk about something called Jordi syndrome. But even apart from the pressure of standing on the pitch as a Cruyff, it was also difficult that we were both working at Barcelona. The choice of whether or not to select him on the pitch always had to be an extremely objective decision.

In Barcelona I was able to keep a close eye on his development, because I wanted to have constant control over three teams: the first, the second and the third. To do that, I needed direct lines of contact with the coaching staff as soon as a player was ready to move up a level. Not least because I've always been of the opinion that you've got to give someone a chance the moment the situation allows it. I didn't care whether he played in the youth team or the second team. It was about putting out players who are good enough. In short: chuck him in and see what happens.

And that's how it was with Jordi, more or less. His quality of play had to be better than anyone else's, though, because the last thing you want as a father is 100,000 people booing your son. Then you've also got the morons shouting that I've been pushing my son up the pecking order. That just wasn't the case. He had to be tough enough to defend himself in the most difficult circumstances.

So my thought process was precisely the opposite of what the idiots were shouting. The moment I decided to give Jordi his debut, a whole trajectory was set out. Until he had reached the level at which he could defend himself against criticism from 100,000 people in the stadium. Or rather: until he could convince all those people that their criticism was misplaced. Football may be a game of mistakes, but someone has to have the quality to rise above them. He's got to be mentally and physically up to the job.

Anyone who thought I was giving my son preferential treatment clearly had no understanding of football. That's why I never allowed it to get to me. The important people to me were the ones who stood by me, the ones I worked with every day, the ones I talked with about the players. So Tonny Bruins Slot, Carles Rexach and I sat down together to ask one question: 'Is he ready? Yes, he's ready. Then he can play.'

And that was that. The squad thought it was the most natural thing in the world as well. They were used to him already. Jordi trained with everyone else, he was often in the changing room, so everyone knew him. But fine, the foundation and the starting point is always quality. Can someone do it or can't they? He could, so he was able to make his debut in the home game against Santander on 10 September 1994.

The person who was most startled was Danny. She hadn't a clue. She was sitting on the terraces, and suddenly she saw Jordi coming out on to the field. Then I was in real difficulties; not at the club, but at home. Luckily it was all great, even excellent. He scored with a diving header after only eight minutes. In the end we won 2–1, Jordi was one of the better players and got a standing ovation.

Unfortunately, when I was fired as trainer in 1996, Jordi had to leave Barcelona too. We'd seen it coming. It was part of the plan to get me out. There was a firm rule at Barcelona designed to prevent a player ending up in the last year of his contract. For that reason all players always had another two or three years to go. That way, during the season there was never any moaning about expiring contracts. Except that didn't happen in Jordi's case. Even though he was one of the young players who had moved from the second team to the first, his contract wasn't changed as it usually would have been following a promotion to a higher level. Since his debut a year earlier, he had regularly made a good impression.

But more and more often, the day before a match – and sometimes also the day after – he had to take a break. All thanks to a doctor who didn't just cock things up, but was also later involved in the fuss about not giving Jordi a new contract. After his operation Jordi didn't hear another word from the board about a new contract. Despite the fact that in December 1995 he'd agreed terms verbally, they never got back to him with a written offer. Every time Jordi tried to chase them up they fobbed him off, saying that they were busy finalizing various details. In April he checked again, but by then it was clear that they'd made the lad a pawn in the political game against me. It was an incredibly cruel situation. Just as I was fired, his contract expired.

Then they tried to claim they held Jordi's registration and we decided to play hardball. Jordi was luckily able to prove that his contract hadn't been extended, which meant that he could leave as a free agent. During a press conference Núñez dragged my son through the mud. The same man who wanted to let my son go announced in public that Jordi had only reached this level thanks to his father, and had used all kinds of tricks so that he could leave as a free agent.

Fortunately, Jordi quickly discovered that good comes from good: manager Alex Ferguson of Manchester United seemed very taken with him. Not least because he had played superbly against United in the Champions League, when we beat them 4–0. So, at the age of twenty-two, Jordi moved to Old Trafford. After the wasps' nest at Barcelona, at last he was in contact with good people again. People like Eric Cantona and David Beckham. Everyone welcomed him with open arms. That's what struck me more than anything over the years. The most talented players almost always seemed to be really good guys. I don't know one extremely good sportsman, in any sport, who comes across as a creep or a bully. They just don't exist. Everyone can think whatever they like about Cantona or Beckham or whoever else happened to be running around there, but all of those guys helped the young lads. That was a very nice feeling. Often when you read the papers, you get opinions or impressions about people, call them what you like. But then you meet them in real life and you don't recognize the person in all those negative stories at all. There isn't a top-level sportsman who's said no when I've asked them a favour.

While our family stayed in Barcelona, in 1996 off Jordi went, out from under my wing. I've never had any difficulties with that. I didn't even go to all his home games. I'd thought about it a lot, but in the end Jordi was standing on his own two feet, and he was released from me. I tried to find a sort of balance. Because, of course, I knew that if I went to see him play at Old Trafford it wouldn't stop there. I'd find myself dealing with the press. Or the manager spontaneously inviting you behind the scenes. For me that's perfectly normal, but by now Jordi was one of his players, not mine. It was a curious situation. You really want to go, but you don't.

Of course, I attended some matches at Old Trafford, where inevitably I ran into Sir Alex Ferguson. Sometimes our contact had to be professional rather than friendly. That often depended on whether the team was playing well or not, whether Jordi had been good or not, and of course whether or not they'd won. Every now and again I had to play hide and seek to avoid an awkward confrontation. Danny and I had also agreed that we wouldn't go to Manchester if it seemed that things at the club weren't going as they were supposed to. Then we would go to the next home game instead.

The same thing happened in 2000, when Jordi moved to Alavés. There the trainer sometimes asked my opinion – just out of interest. The same was true of the chairman, who called out jovially to me to come and sit with him. That's normal, but it's also not normal, because there was always the risk that it would have an effect on my son. I always found those situations difficult, I must honestly admit. At any rate, Jordi had had four lovely years in Manchester. There were good aspects of it for me too. I'd stopped coaching, and had all the time in the world to do what I wanted. Like regularly watching English football, which I really love. I love the brilliant footballing atmosphere they have. Unfortunately I was never able to play there, because of the rule about foreign players that still applied in those days. That was why I thought it was wonderful that Jordi was given that chance, and by England's greatest club as well. My son had been given the chance to do something I hadn't. I thought that was fantastic.

The enjoyment began as soon as I stepped inside Old Trafford. Everyone knew each other. You saw people you'd played against. Bobby Charlton, of course, who was always there. I didn't really know anyone but I felt I knew everyone. That's a crazy feeling, every time. That you're going somewhere where you know everyone. Of course, you know it's not literally the case, but in practice that's how it seems.

It was also great to watch my son on the pitch from up there in the terraces. And I enjoyed the English fans, too. They've got real respect for someone who plays football well. Not just because of that unique talent, but also because he's doing his best, 100 per cent. We don't get that in Holland, or in Spain either, except at Atlético Madrid. At that club, too, people respect someone who gives his all to the match. But English supporters are also hooked on their teams. It's in their DNA. They're always there, in good times and bad. That's why they're good losers too, as long as everyone's really gone for it.

In England Jordi also found the brother that Danny and I couldn't give him. Because that was how we came to see Roberto Martínez. At that time Jordi was playing at

Manchester United and Roberto was at Wigan Athletic. They became bosom pals, and I didn't rule out the possibility of them playing football together one day. At the time they were two lovely young lads, with all their skills. Of course that was all part of it too. Later, my grandson played at Wigan under Roberto for two years. He played in the second team, but it was good for his talent anyway. I regularly went to watch there too, and from close-up you could see that Roberto had come on very well as a manager. He even won the FA Cup, even though Wigan were a relatively small club. With Roberto, too, you can tell straight away that he's a good guy. An open man with an open face.

So, Jordi was doing brilliantly in England. It's also the country where I have my best memory of him as a footballer: his goal for Holland against Switzerland at Villa Park during Euro '96, a game they won 2-0. It's those beautiful moments that have given me a kind of peace. You think: I saw it very clearly, he did it, and he did it at the right moment.

Or what he did at Barcelona in his last match under Rexach. As soon as the game was over, he stepped off the field and said: Bye, I'm off. In fact, that was something extra that he had in his character apart from his footballing qualities. Someone who makes things happen at the moment they have to happen.

Of course, that makes me feel emotional. Sure it does. It's emotion, it's inside. In fact it isn't emotion, it's pride. You barely see it, but I've got it. People saw me on the terrace after that important goal against Switzerland, the way I tried and failed to hurdle the advertising hoarding that time against Sampdoria. Sometimes I just have to do something.

If you take Jordi's whole career, then it was great, then less great, and then not great at all. But in retrospect I was dealing with a fantastic situation. First with myself, then with Jordi. It's wonderful to see him going his own way as a director at Maccabi Tel Aviv, and demonstrating his own way of thinking. And the fact that he's direct. Especially that. If he says something, he's going to follow up on it.

In his way he's doing a huge amount of good stuff. All in the field of honesty. That's his extra strength in the terribly difficult place he is in now. At Maccabi they've got three kinds of players: Jewish, Palestinian and Arab. Everyone lives there and everyone plays there. Jordi's busy trying to put the strongest possible team together, but many of the spectators, who might be Jewish, complain if an Arab or a Palestinian is on the team. When that happens Jordi is the type who defends everyone. I think that this is a supreme kind of education for him.

In the end, in spite of his physical difficulties, Jordi has had a brilliant career. He made the Dutch national team and played at great clubs like Ajax, Barcelona, Manchester United, Alavés and Espanyol. Since then he's also had an amazing chance to do what he wanted to do under the Dutch trainer Co Adriaanse with Metalurh Donetsk in the Ukraine, before giving up as an active footballer in Malta with Valletta FC in 2010 and becoming a manager. Via Malta and Cyprus, he's now in Israel. This all goes to show that Jordi has a very strong character. On the other hand, he used to be a guy with lots of hair, most of which is gone now. I suspect that hurt him more than I realized. That's why it feels really special to me that he's got to where he is today.

I was able to follow every move of Jordi's at Manchester United because for the first time in my life I was no longer active in football. I'd stopped being a player and I'd stopped being a coach. But after that I didn't get bored for a minute. I'm determined to go on evolving; that's always been part of it. As a footballer and a trainer I was always an idealist, so I wanted to apply my experiences to new challenges.

That idea worked from day one. Pretty much everything I came into contact with had something to do with the things I'm good at. Apart from Jordi's matches I had my weekly column in the *Telesport* section of *De Telegraaf*, articles in Spain, and I did commentaries on matches for the Dutch public service broadcaster, NOS. I was also asked to support health clinics. I was busy expanding my horizons and it felt good. I didn't have to do anything else. That's why I actually never missed coaching, not least because it didn't feel good doing something I'd done before. I didn't want to repeat myself, I wanted to move on.

Because I like to look at matters open-eyed, sometimes surprising things cross my path. Like the six-a-side games that I developed with Craig Johnston and Jaap de Groot. Craig is an Australian born in South Africa who ended up in the England squad while at Liverpool. Jaap's mother is American, his father had once been a striker with Ajax, and he spent much of his youth growing up in Texas. So they were both brought up abroad, you might say. They came up with the idea of combining the six-a-side drill with entertainment. That means playing on a smaller pitch, but with goals that are the same size as in normal football. It means you have a lot more goalmouth action, more shots and more scoring.

The football was combined with music, which meant there was something American about it. It was all aimed at entertaining the public and at the same time inspiring young people. I got it straight away. It wasn't just the drill that I'd often had to do during training at Ajax, it was one that I'd later used myself as a coach. In six-a-side you've actually got everything you need. Technique, speed and positional play, because it can be played in three lines and can therefore be transferred to eleven against eleven.

We decided to pour a Cruyff sauce over the rules by making my shirt number 14 run through the games as a kind of thread. For example, a match comprised two seven-minute halves and the field was fifty-six metres long (four times fourteen) and 35.32 metres wide, the 7.32 metres goal width plus fourteen metres on either side. We also came up with all kinds of rules to make the play faster and more attractive. For example, when the ball went out of play you could either throw or kick the ball back in. You couldn't be offside from a throw-in, but you could from a kick-in. Any player receiving a yellow card had to leave the field for two minutes, and couldn't be substituted. A second yellow card had the same effect as a red: dismissal.

One good rule was that a ball-boy had to throw the ball towards the centre spot within ten seconds of a goal being scored. Then the other team could immediately kick off and attack, even if the goal celebrations were still going on.

There were no draws. Because the entertainment factor was very important, a match that was level at full time was decided by a shoot-out. A player started dribbling from the halfway line and had to score within five seconds. A win gave you three points and a defeat zero. The winner of the shoot-out got three points, the loser one.

As you can see, we were all very serious about six-a-side, so it's probably no coincidence that what began as a fun way to train in 1997 would result six years later in the opening of the first Cruyff Court; inner-city football pitches that were built by the Cruyff Foundation to help get more kids playing football. That's struck me on several occasions: I start something, and years later it seems to have been the source of inspiration for a completely new plan. Like with six-a-side.

In the end the six-a-side competition was rolled out on 27 January 1997. We played at the Amsterdam ArenA, Ajax's new stadium which had recently opened, and with Ajax, AC Milan, Liverpool and Glasgow Rangers as participants. The then UEFA president Lennart Johansson thought it was a great idea and had immediately given us his backing.

It was top-level football combined with entertainment originating from the participants' countries. As an extra, we'd set up big screens behind each goal, producing a kind of three-dimensional picture if someone scored. That way a player was shown mid-move. We didn't just want to create a beautiful event, we also wanted to turn it into a live broadcast that would interest the whole world. To that end we brought in CNN and MTV, and it was perfect for a music channel, since during the matches well-known players like

Paul Gascoigne, Paolo Maldini, Steve McManaman and Patrick Kluivert would also talk about music.

It was a great success. About 47,000 spectators in the stadium and millions of TV viewers in more than a hundred countries saw AC Milan winning in the end, after musical performances from the likes of Gerry Marsden, Youssou N'Dour, Massimo Di Cataldo and René Froger.

The six-a-sides also brought me into contact with Peter Brightman, who was in charge of entertainment at ArenA. Peter lived in London, where he was in contact with a group of businessmen who planned to bring top-level football to Ireland. Every week, hundreds of thousands of Irish people were going to England to attend football matches. This had given investors the idea of building a big football stadium in Dublin. The London club Wimbledon, which was still playing in the Premier League at the time but had no stadium of its own, agreed to move to the Irish capital if they got to keep their licence. So at last football-mad Ireland would have its own club in the Premier League.

What attracted me most about the idea was the pacifist ideology behind the project. Because it would be a Premier League club, the idea was that Catholics and Protestants from both sides of the Irish border would support the same team in the stadium, and cheer together when a goal was scored. I thought it was a fascinating idea, setting up a football club in the name of peace during a very violent time. Because of my impartiality, I was asked to be the figurehead. The Catholics and Protestants were at loggerheads, but I was neither, which meant I was an ideal middle-man. I travelled to London a lot to work things out with the investors. I thought it was great. Working on a unique project again, and at the same time hanging out in one of my favourite cities.

Unfortunately, the plan came to a standstill because the Football Association of Ireland didn't want to cooperate. They stuck to the view that if you were playing in Ireland you also had to play in the Irish competition. I thought that was a shame and didn't understand it. Didn't Andorra and Monaco play in the Spanish and French competition? So the problem didn't resolve itself, and even today Ireland has to get by without a top-level club. But OK, I was an experience the richer. In a way, that's happened to me often. You don't know what's happening, but you do know that something's happening.

That was also true of the decision made by a Spanish judge in 1999, three years after I left Barcelona. One of the clauses in my contract was that I had a right to two benefit matches, except the club president Josep Lluís Núñez objected. The court declared that I was within my rights, with the proviso that both matches had to be organized quickly after the ruling. An almost impossible task, but it worked. First on 10 March in Barcelona and then on 6 April in Amsterdam. Two unforgettable evenings.

At Camp Nou, 100,000 spectators could, at long last, show their appreciation for the Dream Team of the early 1990s. Something the players were more than deserving of. For years Núñez had tried to obliterate the memory of that fantastic period, but during the benefit match the fans happily demonstrated what they thought of that. It hasn't often happened to me, but after the final whistle I had goosebumps all over. Particularly when the players gathered around me in the centre circle and I was able to thank the public on behalf of all of us. At that moment

I wasn't thinking, and before I knew it I was singing the club anthem and the whole stadium joined in. A fantastic moment, but the best thing, of course, was that there was finally talk of justice.

I had goosebumps again a month later. While in Barcelona they were still talking about celebrating the Dream Team with the supporters, in Amsterdam the whole of Ajax was affected by it. Players, supporters, tea lady, kit man, ball boys, everybody.

Because Ajax was going to celebrate its centenary a year later, the club didn't want to foreshadow its big anniversary party and decided instead to give the match the theme 'thirty years of finals'. All the players who had ever played in an international final were invited. There were fifty of those, from Piet Keizer to Bryan Roy, from Johan Neeskens to Aron Winter and from Marco van Basten to Dennis Bergkamp. The evening was to be filled with nostalgia. Nothing but football, which is what Ajax stands for. So it opened with the old guard, after that one half of Ajax against FC Barcelona, and the evening closed with forty-five minutes of Ajax International, a team consisting of former Ajax players who now played abroad, against the Spanish champions.

As there had been in Barcelona, there was a big party in Amsterdam. An added bonus was the return of Marco van Basten to the pitch. After being forced to retire aged just thirty while at AC Milan, he'd stayed well clear of the game. His frustration over the recurring ankle injury that had ended his career was still deep-rooted. He had stated that he didn't want to take part, but he would turn up for kick-off. The time came and I couldn't see him anywhere, until play was under way and I suddenly saw Marco standing on the touchline in his football kit. The chemistry of the changing room had apparently grabbed him, and he was ready to muck in. It was a very special moment. First, everything fell silent in ArenA, because the public wasn't sure if it really was Marco, but when they'd worked it out one supporter after another rose to their feet and he got a magnificent ovation from 50,000 fans.

Later that evening in the Hilton Hotel the foundations were laid for another idea. A lot of Ajax players had come to the hotel to chat with everybody. Among them were Søren Lerby and Simon Tahamata, two Ajax players who had watched from the sideline because they had played with other clubs in European finals, but not with Ajax. That was why they hadn't been allowed to play. That left a bad taste in my mouth, because players like that deserved to be on a podium. Then, a few weeks later, I was offered the solution on a plate. I'd told my father-in-law more than once that I wanted to set up my own foundation. It had been in my head since my experiences with the Special Olympics in Washington. I was often asked to contribute to all kinds of charities, but I was rarely told what use my contribution had been, or what had been done with it.

In 1997 I had set up the Johan Cruyff Welfare Foundation, and with the fruits of the benefit match on 6 April I was determined to set it up seriously in Holland at last. First of all with Swiss child-relief agency Terre des Hommes, to learn 'the trade', and partly financed by the Dutch National Postcode Lottery. During one of our brainstorming sessions it was suggested that we set up something that would let top-level football make a gesture towards society. A beautiful, special conclusion to the twentieth century.

In *De Telegraaf*, I would choose the Dutch players of the century, and readers would be able to buy signed pictures of each player selected. The income from the sale of the pictures would finance a youth project in Bijlmer in Amsterdam, and a special present for the Oranje supporters' club.

There was only one problem. However well the pictures sold, they would never be able to cover the total costs. So we needed some kind of an event. A testimonial match in which the best that Dutch football had produced in the twentieth century would be presented to the public once again in the form of the Match of the Century.

It was a magnificent project. On 21 December 1999 the best national coaches and players in Holland's history came together again in the Amsterdam ArenA. They were joined by the best foreign players who had ever played in the Eredivisie. One team was led by Rinus Michels, who had about forty internationals to call upon, from Dennis Bergkamp to the veteran Faas Wilkes. The same applied to the 'foreigners' led by Barry Hughes, with Søren Lerby and Simon Tahamata on the team. The duo who had given us the idea in the first place. It was a worthy farewell to the twentieth century. Whether it was Ove Kindvall, Ralf Edström or Stefan Pettersson; they were all playing in their Feyenoord, PSV and Ajax shirts. Like their other team-mates. Three clubs in one team.

The evening ended with the present from the players to the Oranje supporters' club: the unveiling of twelve sculptures of the best eleven Dutch players of the century and the best national coach. Rinus Michels, Edwin van der Sar, Ruud Krol, Ruud Gullit, Frank Rijkaard, Johan Neeskens, Wim van Hanegem, Abe Lenstra, Marco van Basten, Piet

Keizer, Faas Wilkes and I were cast in bronze, and all of us still stand by the entrance to the KNVB sport centre in Zeist. The net receipts from the Match of the Century came to about a million guilders. Enough to build the Oranjehorst multi-function sport complex in Bijlmer. The funds left over went to the Johan Cruyff Welfare Foundation. But just as great was the message that we'd delivered with the internationals, by showing everyone that so much more can be done in the name of sport.

We were always trying to think up ways of setting things in motion. One good example of that was the Winter Ball. Along with Jaap de Groot and the cabaret artist Raoul Heertje, I'd devised a plan to organize a football match in a theatre. We just came up with it on the spur of the moment, from the idea that extremely good footballers are actually artists, and therefore suited to the theatre as well. At first we laughed about it, until it actually came about in June 2003.

The venue was the Concertgebouw in Amsterdam, after a farewell celebration for Aron Winter, who had made his debut under me at Ajax. His old teammate Frank Rijkaard had been a bit worried about how Aron would end his career. Proof once again that footballers never let each other down. Pretty much all the players with whom Aron had played at Ajax, Lazio, Inter Milan and the Dutch squad made free time for his farewell ceremony. From Marco van Basten to Ronaldo, and from Paul Ince to Roberto Di Matteo. To play not in a stadium, but in one of the most beautiful theatres in Holland. Textiles technology group Royal TenCate laid an artificial grass mat twenty-five metres square, on which a game could be played in the big auditorium of the Concertgebouw. The four hundred guests were seated in the Concertgebouw's orchestra pit, and the Dutch Opera, as 'supporters', created the right atmosphere during matches inspired by Aron's career.

The evening began with a match between the 1987 Ajax team that I'd coached against the Dutch squad led by Rinus Michels that won the 1988 European Championship. After that came Lazio vs. Inter Milan and the programme ended with Louis van Gaal's Ajax against the Black Ties. The Black Ties played in a black shirt with a bow tie. Another original idea that was the perfect kit for very special footballers like Ronaldo, Clarence Seedorf and Patrick Kluivert. Because Aron wanted to end his career with a gift to the community, we decided to use the Winter Ball as a kick-off for a new project by my foundation: the Cruyff Courts. The artificial grass surface in the Concertgebouw was perfect for the first Cruyff Court in Aron's home town, Lelystad.

The Winter Ball was a fantastic evening. Every player came on to the pitch along a red carpet, and the referee was in a tuxedo. The whole world would talk about the event. It was broadcast on CNN, and even the *International Herald Tribune* wrote a great article about it. Of course, these are more than just nice memories, because a few so-called festive evenings led to really serious things. The six-a-sides sowed the seed for the Cruyff Court programme, and the testimonial game at Ajax and the Match of the Century put the Cruyff Foundation seriously on the map, while it was partly thanks to the Winter Ball that the first Cruyff Court was laid. These days you can find those pitches all over the world. Not playing any more, but staying busy with all kinds of things and achieving that bit extra. It can be that simple.

*

My experience with football club directors has been a lot less fun. To my mind, I've always shown good will, even after they stopped me working as a coach and put me on the sidelines. Put it this way: sometimes your connection with the club is better than it is at other times. It has a lot to do with the board members. I've always got on famously with Michael Praag at Ajax and Joan Laporta at Barcelona, for example. In 1999 Ajax named me as an honorary club member. When that happens, you can do one of two things: either you just play the role of honorary member by virtue of wearing the badge, or else you try to use that status to bring added value to the club. But when you notice that other people inside the club have different thoughts about that value, in the end you have to go back to just wearing the badge again.

During that time I took a couple of knocks from the Ajax board. The first came with the appointment of Co Adriaanse, and then when Louis van Gaal was taken on as technical director. Twice I was approached, ostensibly to give advice, but twice I later found out that everything had been decided already, and I'd just been used for show.

When I was asked in 2000 to name a suitable candidate for manager, I mentioned Frank Rijkaard. Frank had done excellent work as coach for the Dutch team, and should really have taken them through to win that year's European Championship. We'd been knocked out in the semi-final, missing two penalties in normal time against Italy and then a few more during the penalty shoot-out. But the team had played fantastic football. Hence my choice of Rijkaard.

I discovered later that, a few weeks before my discussion, an agreement had already been made with Co Adriaanse. Let me say first of all, I've got nothing against

Adriaanse, but that's all I can say about it. When I protested, the club management announced through the media that Ajax's interests took precedence over everything else. But who actually determines what's in Ajax's interest? If it's done in the same high-handed way as I was overruled, then I can't say I'm wild about it. Three years later the same thing happened again during the appointment of the club's new technical director. Ronald Koeman had done outstanding work as a coach, but later the board asked me what I thought about the job of technical director, and who I saw as a possible candidate.

During that discussion the director Arie van Eijden and the chairman John Jaakke asked three times if I was against the idea of appointing Louis van Gaal, and three times I answered that it wasn't a matter of whether I was for or against van Gaal, it was about the kind of technical director that Ajax most needed at that moment, and I didn't think van Gaal was the right fit. I tried to make that clear with all kinds of examples. But yes, if the choice has already been determined, of course there are all kinds of ways of pretending to consider my opinions.

Van Gaal was appointed, but when he himself claimed to have been chosen for the job months before my advice was sought, that was the limit. He even seemed to agree with some of the examples I had used in support of my vision for the club. So the question is why the directors had to play games like that? Why was I suddenly an advisor, why did I suddenly have to consider the merits of potential technical directors when the appointment had been done and dusted?

I was absolutely furious when I heard that, before I'd been consulted, the choice of van Gaal had already been discussed in all sections of the club. All the yes men had been brought onside first before involving anyone else in what would now be a losing battle.

The worst failing was that a purely technical decision was being made by people who didn't have the necessary abilities, but were supposedly acting in the interests of Ajax. Just as it was in the interests of Ajax that van Gaal and I should make peace with each other. But why should I? They'd left me out and got on with doing their thing. All else apart, there wasn't a single reason to change Koeman's working situation, because he was doing brilliantly. But the club management thought that Koeman and his assistants Ruud Krol and Tonny Bruins Slot were isolating themselves too much, which meant that the board didn't know enough about what was going on inside the team. I empathized with the coaching team, after my experiences with Núñez in Barcelona. Another director who wanted to force his way into the changing room.

With the appointment of van Gaal the directors hoped to get more of a grip on Koeman, under whom Ajax had become both league champions and KNVB Cup winners in 2002 and had reached the quarter finals of the Champions League in 2003. As happened to me in 1987 after winning the Cup Winners' Cup, something that was good was broken from above. Within a year they'd brought it off. Van Gaal had resigned in frustration and the same was true of Koeman. Both the victims of boardroom games. Thought up by people who are still involved with Ajax. But as far as I'm concerned they aren't Ajax. I love the club I grew up with. That's Ajax for me. So all problems and frustrations slide off me as soon as I walk into the canteen. If I go there,

I know in advance that it's going to be nice. That still means a lot to me. The rest they can keep.

The same is true of Barcelona. Where directors are once again a part of the political game within Catalonia. I never joined in there. Even though, particularly during the Franco era, I played along when they demanded that you spoke out in favour of Barcelona and against Madrid. A point of view like that matters. The problem for me was that I just kept being involved in things that were really too much for me. I was still too young, too apolitical, completely uneducated, or whatever you want to call it. It wasn't until late 1974 that I started getting a handle on it. Thanks to the board member Armand Carabén, who had a superior intelligence and was very good at explaining why things happened, and why there were differences of opinion. It started with the Catalan language, which was forbidden by Madrid. And not just the spoken language; Catalan names were forbidden as well. As I've said, we noticed that when we were told not to call our son Jordi. We found that unacceptable. Things like that are completely outside our way of thinking.

But in Barcelona, too, I didn't let anyone force anything down my throat. I behaved exactly as I'd grown up in Amsterdam, as a kid after the war. Everyone in my generation was influenced by the Beatles, who were different and did their own thing. I did the same in the field of sport and football. That clashed with the situation inside Catalonia. There were lots of attitudes in the region that I wanted to understand, but even though I thought about them a lot, I still didn't understand them.

Carabén was the first person to tell me not to give up. Then I said again, 'But this is ridiculous.' 'That's true,'

Carabén replied, 'but it's how they were brought up.' Later former Dutch environment minister Pieter Winsemius said the same thing: 'You don't even agree with it and I don't even agree with it. But that man's been there for twenty years and that's how he was brought up. He's just doing what he was raised to do. And we don't think it's OK, that's what we think, and that's how it is, but you can't blame them. All you can do is try and change things.' It was people like Carabén and Winsemius who suggested the nuanced ways in which I finally understood such problems.

That's how I look at the situation in present-day Catalonia. Just as it was forty years ago, the debate is about whether to separate from the rest of Spain. It's fifty–fifty. In other words, in the case of partition the people are divided. Is that what you want?

As a Dutchman, of course, I'm used to the polder model of building consensus between opposing views. Always waffling on and then coming together in the end. They've never had that in Spain. No one's ever been willing to water things down. Absolutely nobody. Not the ones who want to separate, not the ones who want to stay together and not the ones in Madrid. But if you haven't got a majority, you should work together. And if you have to work together, you should also look into the other person's problems. That's why it's very interesting to read the political reports. To see who gets that in the end.

Then I see the attitude of certain political party leaders who think 'without me you can't form a coalition to govern the country, so I want my portion of the cake'. But it's wrong to want the whole cake for yourself. You mustn't be greedy. Instead, take a step back and try to think on the basis of the whole people. Put yourself in their position. It seems to me that in that case you'll probably conclude that the opposing sides aren't all that far apart. I follow it all, but, of course, I don't really understand any of it.

And yet some things strike me as ridiculous. Learning a lot of languages is the best form of education for your children, so that they can communicate with everyone. To optimize their general development. But often it's determined that one hour is enough. Why not two or three hours? It's incredibly precious for someone to have command of another language, at least that's how it seems to me. When I was growing up I was always told, 'Son, go and travel and learn your languages so that you can communicate with everyone. Because if you can talk to everyone, you can create understanding.'

I became the coach of the Catalan national side in November 2009. For me, that was not a political appointment, but in the end that's what it became. It was actually a mix of a whole pile of things. First of all, it shouldn't be an official function. It's about a match between A and B, and I'm the trainer of one of the two teams. But in practice, you end up with other things becoming a part of it. At the end of the ride, when politicians started paying our team more and more attention, everything was given a bigger political charge. I think that really shouldn't happen. It's better to think very carefully about how regional divisions are dealt with. Of course, it's great to reinforce Catalan pride. There's nothing at all wrong with that. But you must never lose sight of the sporting aspect. The stadium will be full of Catalans, but they can't just come for the flag, they have to come for the football as well.

Because the Catalan squad only gains in strength as long as there are good footballers in it. If you lose them, any other effect of the team is suddenly reduced. So politics has significance only when the sports side of things works. And that is reliant on lots of things. Just take footballers: they are immersed in their own club's season, and the most important thing for the leading players isn't politics. Perhaps they think about politics, but on match days they're also trying to avoid getting injured. So all the politics or whatever else surrounding the game is all well and good, but the only questions that really matter to them are: how will I approach the match, how am I going to win it and how do I not get injured. That was how I thought as a national coach as well. There was a lot of song and dance about the importance of national pride, but if someone breaks or sprains something, you've got a real problem on your hands.

I have a lot of sympathy with the Catalan cause, but first of all I'm a Dutchman. That's still the case. I don't keep my mouth shut, and I do whatever I feel like doing. With all the usual constraints. I don't lurk somewhere at the back. I am reasonably clear headed, and when something happens I don't pronounce on it from the point of view of the Catalan or the Dutchman, but from my own standpoint. From the freedom of thought that's part of every Dutch citizen's birthright. Of course it's a very important given, that you can be free in your head to think what you like. That I don't have to be scared that, if I say something out of line, then this or that will happen. That attitude has given me problems with a lot of directors. It cost me my jobs at Ajax and Barcelona, but both the men in charge later had to face their own shortcomings. They both put their clubs in difficulties again.

Where that's concerned, Barcelona can be very grateful to Joan Laporta. He became president in 2003, and while the then management of Ajax had their eye on me as an advisor, he was quite open with me about what was going on. It all started when Laporta asked me early on about whom he should appoint as trainer and technical director. When the positions were filled by Frank Rijkaard and Txiki Begiristain, they held the club up to the light. A lot of former players were taken on as advisors. No committee was called on to advise and review the decision, which meant that it all worked quickly and efficiently. And Laporta and I got out of their way.

Barcelona now enjoys the benefit of that.

9

I'm a child of Ajax, and I've come to love Barcelona. That's why for the last ten years I've been involved in the re-organization of both clubs. Barcelona asked me and Ajax happened to me. In Barcelona it worked for three years, in Ajax it didn't because they weren't 100 per cent behind the reorganization. It doesn't work without full commitment. That's a question of adding up the numbers as well. One big difference is that Ajax is a business whose shares are traded on the stock market, and Barcelona is still a club in private hands. In Amsterdam you're dealing with directors and commissioners, and in Barcelona with a president. He works a lot more directly, because there are no shareholders to answer to. The system at Ajax involves a lot more pro-cedures, and that means you need more time as well.

Remarkably, the whole business with Barcelona and, in the end, Dream Team II, started with the player I actually had my first clash with. But after his unsettling departure from Ajax in 1987, Frank Rijkaard and I have grown closer and closer. I think that the formation of such relationships is a matter of time. Eventually you reach a certain kind of peace which means you can somehow move on to the next phase of your life.

Put it like this: we've both learned from it. When we fell out, we were each at the start of something, he as a player, me as a coach. But after that we developed in our different ways. Frank certainly did, both as a player and as a coach. That was why it was great that I was able to advise Joan Laporta to take him on as coach at Barça. Not just because I think highly of Frank, but also because I know what he can do.

Because, to be perfectly clear, at Barcelona's level you don't make allowances. You can't. Not for the club and not for the person who is doing the job, whatever job it is. That's why I thought very hard about the situation at Barcelona. What did the club need, and what did the new coach need to do? Frank met all the criteria. In terms of his image, the way he speaks, and most importantly he'd played at the top level. That's his footballing side, which is beyond question. And he has charisma, and had a good assistant in the form of Henk ten Cate. Henk is another coach I've always followed with great interest, because wherever he worked, something was always happening. I love that. He and Frank had a good balance between them.

However, the big advantage was that, as a president, Laporta was actually always pushing footballers forward and always letting the footballers take the footballing decisions. Laporta was the Barcelona president from 2003 to 2010, and in all those years he was actually the exception to the rule. He was not the kind of person who says, 'I'm the president, so I make the decisions.' He was very clear to us about that: 'This is a problem, let's sit down and solve it.' So he was someone who thought just the same way as we did. He was excellent in that respect, and Laporta also has the honour of having set the process of Dream Team II in motion. That whole series of achievements.

After I'd put forward the names of Frank Rijkaard and Txiki Begiristain as trainer and technical director, he went into action straight away and things were sorted out very quickly. That's exactly as it should be. I'm always surprised at the way people judge trainers, and who are the ones to do so. That's why you also always see big blunders being committed in choices like that. Decisions being made by board members or directors who haven't a clue what the primary considerations should be in making those decisions. As discussed earlier, this means they're made on the basis of interviews and lobbying in boardrooms and directors' offices.

So someone can be a fantastic youth trainer, but a disastrous head coach. Or someone can succeed at a second-rate club, but fall through the ice right at the top. And vice versa. A trainer who gets it right at the top level may not make it at a small club. Just as not every head coach is automatically going to be a skilled technical director as well. What I'm trying to say is that in the field of coaches, a deep understanding of the human psyche is required to put the right person in the right place. That's why I'm always perplexed when I see the way in which lots of clubs deal with challenges like that. Bad choices can have huge consequences, often leading to damage whose effects last for years.

Different posts require different qualities. A youth trainer must be able to bring people on. The great danger during that 'bringing on' is that the youth trainer will just break the player's old habits rather than polishing up the new talent. An example. If you've got someone who dribbles too much, you don't stop him dribbling, instead you put him up against a big, physically strong opponent. If he's subjected to a few crunching tackles, he'll soon learn all by himself that he's got to pass the ball. And, of course, boys in early adolescence need a different approach from young men of sixteen or seventeen who are on the threshold of the first team. You can't just dump a youth trainer on them.

Similarly, you can't just appoint any head coach. The trainer must be a good fit for the club. A club that's at the top, or in mid-table, or at the bottom, often require three totally different types of trainer. Not only is the difference in the quality of the players enormous, you're also dealing with a completely different range of challenges. A technical director, once again, is someone who seeks out and guards the threads of history and tradition that run through the club, and who must act as a conduit between the board-room and the pitch. It's absolutely fatal for an organization if a technical director ignores those lines and follows his own plan.

That's why I'm always hugely irritated when I see an appointment made that clearly isn't going to work. Then you often have the problem of the decision-makers leaving things as they are for far too long, to avoid looking like idiots. By the time the decision is finally revoked, it's often too late and the club has to pick up the pieces.

That wasn't the case at Barcelona, even though Rijkaard got off to a tough start. That wasn't so strange, and I wasn't surprised, either. If you want something to change com-pletely, you can't expect it to work within a few weeks. Of course, I was in contact with him during that phase. That's no more than usual. Friends always try to help each other when it comes to the crunch. But to be completely clear on the matter: there was no question of meddling in technical management on my part. In spite of the difficult start, things were in good hands with Frank. He had grown up with our system of play at Ajax and there, thanks to what he had learned while with AC Milan, he was able to add his own insights. He also brought an enormous amount of experience. For me he's one of the best all-round footballers I've ever seen. He could defend with the best of them, he organized the midfield and still had scoring potential. All of that in one person, who also had the right mentality and a good set of brains. The fact that he called me every now and again to sound me out only serves to underline his professionalism.

That was also typical of Barcelona under Laporta. Because of all the politics that went on inside and around the club, Barcelona was always a rumbling volcano. Joan did great work in controlling all the political issues and ensuring the coaches and players remained unaffected by them. Which meant that they could focus on building up the team.

And look at the result. Within a few months it started working, the public started to believe in it and the results came in. Most crucially, a footballing foundation had been laid once more, setting up Barcelona as a model. The most important thing was standing side by side at difficult times. Loyalty when it's really called for. That's an absolute necessity at clubs like Ajax and Barcelona. Not just at bad times, but when things are going well, too.

About four months into Rijkaard's first season, 2003–04, accusations began to surface that I was throwing my weight around. That I would even drop in to the changing room from time to time and bombard the club with advice. In fact, I'd only been to Camp Nou twice since Frank was appointed, I'd never turned up at the changing room, certainly not during a match, and I'd spoken to the technical director precisely once. Even then we hadn't talked about players, so I'd said nothing about transfers either. They still put all that stuff in the media, though. And not just in the newspapers. First they write all kinds of nonsense, and then it's discussed like a factual news item on radio and TV programmes. It's always the same old routine, every time. In spite of the fact that Rijkaard's squad was playing better and better football.

The truth was much less interesting. Both the trainer and the president are good friends of mine. If they've got issues that concern them, sometimes they'll call me to ask my opinion. Simple as that. But part of the Catalan press thought this was quite wrong. It was bad for the club. That the criticism I offered had nothing to do with football, but was made solely to gain influence. So they tried to play us off against each other. But OK, that's all part and parcel of FC Barcelona, and the trick is for everyone concerned to keep a cool head. In that respect Laporta always set a good example, and also ensured stability within the club.

It was striking that during the initial phase of Rijkaard's tenure, when there was the greatest danger of things going wrong, Laporta's future successor seemed to be the weak link. Laporta had brought in Sandro Rosell as a vice-president, but the pair soon clashed because Rosell wanted to drop Rijkaard after only a few months. As a Nike executive, Rosell had spent time in Brazil. There he had formed a good relationship with the Brazilian national coach Luiz Felipe Scolari, whom he wanted to bring to Barcelona.

Rosell was part of a small group who had decided that they wanted to take Barcelona off in a new direction, and to do that they needed a certain type of coach and technical director. Rijkaard was struggling, but the choice had been made very clear, and you have to stick to that. When success didn't come immediately, Rosell was ready to change course after a few months, and go for a completely different type of coach, and hence also for another style of football. When the team eventually started to do well, of course, he was on his own. Rijkaard never forgot Rosell's attitude when he'd needed the support from above. Rosell was a jamming station in the whole process, and after two years he threw in the towel and resigned.

Over five years Frank, Henk ten Cate and later Johan Neeskens did a fantastic job. Not only did they win the European Cup again in 2006, fourteen years after the Dream Team, but their way of playing football had become more refined as well. This was a line that Frank's successor, Pep Guardiola, would go on pursuing from 2008 onwards. In 2007 Pep had got the necessary trainer's diploma and was immediately appointed coach of Barcelona B. Once again Barcelona were proving that attractive football can also deliver results. The impact of such stylish successes is all the greater too, because millions of football lovers want to enjoy the game as well as the result. They want to enjoy the beauty that our sport has to offer. Frank and Pep brought that about, and in so doing left the most beautiful legacy imaginable at Barcelona.

In March 2010 I saw that with my own eyes. All of a sudden I received a call from Barcelona, telling me that I'd been unanimously voted in as honorary president. When something like that happens, you wonder why. It seemed to have everything to do with how I'd influenced and changed football both at Barcelona and in Spain. As a player and, above all, as a coach. I was responsible for introducing a style of football that had extended to the Spanish national squad. Such compliments are not just great to hear, they make you proud as well. But the way Barcelona was run under Laporta had a lot to do with it as well. The management always made me feel that my ideas were being considered seriously, even if they weren't all adopted without further ado. That's only sensible. To have my own way completely is the last thing I'd want.

We just treated each other honestly, like adults. That was why I was always ready to help later on when they wanted to talk. Whether it was about the attitude of a new trainer or giving free shirt sponsorship to Unicef. That one was particularly contentious, but I thought it was an excellent initiative. It was an action that radiated style, just the right kind of thing for a club like Barcelona. A similar philosophy applied to the managerial appointments first of Frank and later of Pep, two footballers I'd worked with when I was coach at Ajax and Barcelona. When Laporta asked me why he ought to appoint them, I told him that, as well as knowing what kind of football suited the club, they would also provide an image of calm and intelligent management.

It's clear to see what I meant by that. It's not just that Guardiola is a winning manager, it's more about the way he wins, and the stylish way he goes about it. Like Rijkaard, he's a great example for young people. A hugely positive presence who always rubs off on the clubs he manages.

During Laporta's presidency I felt very much at home at Barcelona. Both head coaches – Rijkaard and Guardiola – and the technical director had played under me, and I already had a bond with the president before he was elected. They're all people who grew up with Barcelona. And that was apparent in the contract discussions as well. Guardiola settled for a relatively low salary, and just earned a bit more once the team had won a few trophies. The fact that he was happy to do that showed Guardiola to be a Barcelona man first, and only then a coach. I learned that formula at Ajax, by the way. I grew up in Amsterdam with the principle of a low basic salary and high win bonuses. That way the club doesn't spend money it hasn't yet earned. And it's how you stay financially sound personally.

It was brilliant to learn that such a system could be implemented at Barcelona as well. The club naturally made its own policies, but also gave me the feeling that my opinion counted for something. So I wasn't just directly involved with the club, I also felt responsible for it. That was apparent in Guardiola's attitude as well. It's about the club first and foremost, in the knowledge that, if the club's OK, everything else follows on. It felt really good to be the honorary president of an organization like that.

But that wasn't how things continued. A few months after I was made honorary president, Joan Laporta had reached the end of his term, and the club members, or *socios*, chose Sandro Rosell as his successor. That brought politics back into the club. Only a few weeks after his election, in July 2010, I was forced to resign as honorary president. When I read in the paper that the new board had put my position on the agenda for the first meeting, I was immediately on my guard. Then when I heard that the new president had persuaded the club to take counsel's advice regarding whether the award had been made in line with the rules of the club, I immediately drew my own conclusions and stepped down.

There was talk of revenge by the new president against previous board members, and all of a sudden off went the political fireworks inside Barcelona again. Even someone as resourceful as Pep Guardiola couldn't do anything about it, and I wasn't surprised when he decided to leave Barcelona two years later, in spite of their continuing success. But luckily Guardiola's policy was by then so fully anchored in the club that it will hopefully keep on working for years. His system of play has become a significant part of the club philosophy.

That was exactly what I'd planned to do myself when I started at the club in 1988, at which time it was a big club, with a lot of money, but no prizes and colourless football. It's great to see everyone passing on the baton. First from me to Rijkaard and then from Frank to Pep, who continued the process in a fantastic way, in his very own way. It is an ideology that has turned Barcelona into an institution. A club that symbolizes a unique philosophy in football.

10

Of course, it would have been fantastic if Ajax had grown in the same way that Barcelona have done. Particularly because Ajax had several years' advantage in footballing philosophy thanks to my old managers Jany van der Veen and Rinus Michels, who brought a perfect combination of technical development and professionalism to the club. Even though I'd been messed around as an advisor by Ajax more than once, in 2008 I agreed to reorganize the youth training set-up. Marco van Basten had been brought in as first-team manager, but when it came to it he wasn't able to roll out his vision as he'd hoped.

The biggest problem he faced was that, to do so, he'd have to start by replacing various coaches, which didn't go down well. It was suggested that relations between Marco and me were strained, because of our difference of opinion over approaches to training, although at that point that wasn't the case. Though terms had been agreed in February, Marco wasn't due to start until after the Euros that summer, but for both practical and ethical reasons I wanted to sort things out before 1 April, since it was only fair that the trainers in question should know how things stood. Then they would have plenty of time to look for other jobs, and Ajax could bring in the right people to keep developing the philosophy of the club and evolve the kind of football style I thought we should be playing. If that wasn't done before the start of April the rules said you had to go through the next season with the staff unchanged, and that would be a waste of precious time. Marco thought it was all going too quickly, and didn't agree with me on the best course of action to take when hiring the new staff, so when I couldn't convince him I dropped out. Of course, I was very disappointed about it, but it would show great poverty of spirit if that had drawn a line under our friendship.

After that my involvement with Ajax declined. Every couple of months I'd call in at Sportpark De Toekomst, Ajax's youth academy and training facility, usually to watch the reserves or the A1 juniors play, or to take in a training session. Before and after that I'd go to chat with the players in the refectory. In the old days we'd always talked about going 'out the back', by which we meant Sportpark Voorland, the area behind De Meer Stadion where the lower elevens trained and played and which was little more than some fields and a canteen. It was really far too small, and when the club left De Meer for the ArenA the facilities moved with it. Nowadays, 'the back' means De Toekomst, which was, after all, more or less behind the stadium, albeit a couple of kilometres away. It was there that I always met the people I'd grown up with at Ajax, the people who are the club as far as I'm concerned, and the people I felt cherished the spirit of the club as I remember it as both player and manager.

At that table, just like at Voorland in the past, football was always the central topic of discussion, sometimes with heated debates about how the situation at Ajax could be improved. It was around about this time that the players and the staff started suggesting that things were not going well, and that more and more of the 'Ajax philosophy' was being abandoned. It was now well over ten years since we had been one of the top European sides, and although home attendances were stable at around 50,000, none of us could understand how easily people inside the club had put distance between them and the core values on which the club had been built.

By 2008, I was also getting more and more irritated by the insistence of the national team's coaching staff that Holland's positional play and technical skill were fantastic, whereas, in truth, the national side were playing very poorly and without imagination. Tears sometimes filled my eyes when I saw the uninspiring techniques some Dutch footballers used to stay at the top of the game without giving the fans what they wanted. And it wasn't just the players; the coaches were equally guilty. They were making formation an ever-greater problem, while in fact it's so simple: when you have possession you make the field big and when you lose the ball you make it small again. That's a fundamental principle that you can learn in childhood. Players can be made familiar with it from a very early age, but if you keep bringing footballers into the team who weren't taught that principle in their training, then it becomes a problem. You start to see defenders running back towards their own goal when they lose the ball, rather than moving forward to put pressure on the player in possession. That can cause problems for the whole squad: if a defender retreats too quickly, the midfield is thrown into confusion and in the end the attackers are isolated as well. Such misjudgements create a loss of balance, and the whole shape of the side disintegrates. This was the style of play that I was seeing both at Ajax and from the national team, and it was disheartening to watch. We spent many hours at De Toekomst arguing over these issues and the best ways to repair the damage that was being caused to the game we loved.

As far as I could see, the root of the problem lay with the training methods at Ajax, because, as before under Michels, the national team were taking their inspiration for how to train and how to play from the training ground at Ajax. The club was clinging to a particular vision that was ugly and outdated, and the national squad was trained in that spirit, but with little focus on improving individual talent. Too much time during training was spent working as a group, based on the club vision, with far too little emphasis on one-to-one training sessions to hone particular skills. Added to which, the decline in street football of the kind I'd played as a kid meant that a young player was now working on his fundamental techniques about ten hours a week less, and over the course of even a few years that really makes a big difference. The result was that flair players were becoming increasingly rare, which had a very negative effect on how enjoyable games were for the fans.

Players were also suffering from a lack of individually tailored training, not only at Ajax but also at other clubs, which explains why a lot of Dutch footballers find themselves in difficulties as soon as the plan breaks down and they're thrown back on their own resources. You see that not just in the first eleven, but also in the youth teams below them, although in the youth team it doesn't surface so quickly because the play at that level is slower. It's a different story at the top. Once an opponent finds their weak spot, a lot of players haven't a clue what to do and they get found out very quickly. That was one of the reasons why neither Ajax nor Holland had been at the top of European football for so long. As a fan you stand there dumbfounded, watching professionals completely losing their ability between one move and the next. Playing with team spirit is one thing, but if you don't also focus on the players' own strengths, the fans are going to notice. And it was this failure not only to concentrate on basic skills, but also to acknowledge that there was even a problem, that was driving a wedge between me and the club I had been part of since I was ten years old, and that had been a part of me even longer. As you can imagine, that hurt me deeply.

At Ajax, failure to concentrate on individual skills had started a while back, around 2000 I would say, but got steadily worse as the years went on. By 2008 there was no decent football being played, there was no unity among the trainers, and at one point an agent even appeared to have an office of his own at De Toekomst, from where he could persuade players aged thirteen, fourteen and fifteen to sign for him. But it wasn't until September 2010 that the bomb went off.

The previous season Ajax had qualified for the Champions League as runners-up in the Eredivisie, and had been drawn in the same group as Real Madrid. Like all the fans, I'd been looking forward to the games between them. Real Madrid vs. Ajax is a classic, a match with great historical status. I wasn't the only one eagerly awaiting our trip to Spain, the whole world was, but on the night I saw the worst Ajax ever. The score was 2–0 but it might just as easily have been 12–0. I let rip in my weekly column in *Telesport*:

This is No Longer Ajax

Last week I saw Ajax playing a weaker opponent (Willem II) and a stronger one (Real Madrid). Let's not beat around the bush: this Ajax is even worse than the team from the time before Rinus Michels joined the club in 1965.

Two and a half years ago the Coronel report came out, with all kinds of conclusions and suggestions for the future. If you take a look at all the things that came out of that, it's one big drama. In terms of finance, in terms of training, scouting, procurement and in terms of football. What Ajax showed against both Willem II and Real no longer had anything to do with the standards that the club has always stood for.

In the build-up, Real–Ajax was still being heralded as a unique match between two historic clubs. Two teams who have enriched international football with their playing. Instead, Ajax delivered the greatest disgrace in the club's history. After the final result everyone was happy that it was 'only' 2–0, while it could just as well have been 8–0 or 9–0. Then there was all that nonsense about boys and men, when in fact there was absolutely no age difference between the two teams. The football and Ajax's attitude just weren't up to it.

I honestly admit that I feel a lot of sorrow, because this is no longer Ajax. This team is no longer in a position to play the ball to each other more than three times, and in Madrid they had one shot at goal. With about six players trained by the club, almost all of them hopeless.

So the fact that the club is at the top of the Eredivisie doesn't mean much to me, because there's nothing wrong with my eyesight. Meanwhile the general manager Rik van den Boog is announcing that the training is great, they're buying three strikers all of the same type and they don't have any wingers. Just as, two and a half years after his report, the chairman Uri Coronel has introduced a policy that hasn't led to improvement in any area. I have come to the same conclusion as I did two and a half years ago: Ajax needs a great big broom. Back then I myself wanted to apply rigorous changes to youth training, except that in the end the people I was counting on couldn't put them into effect. With all the consequences that you see today.

There's also the fact that the club has been turned into one big fifth column. That starts with the members' council, which you would expect to include specialists in every area in the club. Now it consists mostly of pals and acquaintances covering each other's backs. In turn, it's from that members' council that the board of directors is assembled, which also has a majority in the commissioners' council, which in the end appoints the directors.

So from members' council to management there's a red thread of people covering for each other, while the club sinks further and further. They've all run off with the family silver. So in the interests of the club they should all leave. And then the club should start over, just as it did in 1965. Then Ajax took its two best decisions ever, by appointing Rinus Michels as head coach and involving Jany van der Veen more closely in training and scouting. Two people who hadn't just grown up with Ajax, but who also knew what the club represented, and what was needed to turn Ajax into Ajax again. Little remains of their life's work. For an 'Ajacied'* like me that really hurts.

---

* devoted Ajax fan

I knew that there would be major consequences from sticking my neck out like this, and everything that subsequently happened in my relationship with Ajax started with the reaction to that match, but I don't regret saying it – it was time that someone said something and tried to sort out the mess of a team that Ajax had become. Later it was suggested that this was a power grab, an attempted coup, which is complete nonsense. It had nothing at all to do with power, and everything to do with the fury I was feeling about how my club was throwing away the legacy that had been built up since Michels took over in the 1960s. That loss unleashed a huge force within me, although admittedly I was overwhelmed by the effect of it.

I can't count the number of people who tried to get in touch with me after they had watched the match, and we all felt exactly the same way. They included a lot of former players, and so I decided to use my column to send out a rallying cry – to bring the forces together to try to fix this sorry mess. That gave some people the impression that I was trying to break Ajax. But they didn't understand. It wasn't about breaking the club – quite the opposite. It was about repairing it. That was why I went into action, because I no longer recognized my Ajax. Not just on the pitch, off it as well. Rather than a club that gave off warmth, it had become a club full of opposition and opponents.

Of course, no one needed to tell me how complex the solution to the problem would be, but I found that out later. Essentially, though, it wasn't all that difficult. If you looked at who represented the club, you immediately saw that there was a lack of football knowledge there. There wasn't a single former first-team player on the commissioners' council, the board, the members' council or the club administration. Not one! So it wasn't at all surprising that the club was failing to play decent football – the administrators didn't have the first clue about the tactics and techniques that the club had been built on. That was why I appealed to all Ajacieds to join forces quickly and put forward candidates for the next members' council election. On 14 December 2010 eight of the twenty-four seats were being contested, and new candidates could be nominated before 30 November. This was a chance to take a first important step using the democratic route, by appointing Ajacieds like Marc Overmars, Tscheu La Ling, Edo Ophof, Peter Boeve, Keje Molenaar and others. I'm deliberately mentioning these names to show that not all footballers are as stupid as some people still claim.

Someone like Overmars, who had played at Ajax, Arsenal and Barcelona, had helped to turn Go Ahead Eagles, who were then in the second-tier Eerste Divisie, into one of the three professional clubs which, according to the KNVB, were in perfect financial health. Just as Ling in Slovakia had completely reorganized AS Trenčín along the lines of the 'old' Ajax. Ophof, Boeve and Molenaar had also done excellent work, and I could name various others too, but what mattered was that these people had the right kind of experience on and off the pitch to help get Ajax back to where we wanted it to be, and take the club to the top of European football again.

I wasn't just concerned with getting players into the club management. It was about creating a better relationship between former players and specialists in the field of finance, marketing and PR. After getting players into the Ajax management, that had to be the next step, because the situation was that commissioners and the administrators didn't have a top-level footballing background, but they still had to decide who would be the best coach or director. In a situation like that, the directors should be able to turn to the members' council for advice, except that even they had no understanding of top-level football. So, first of all, more 'football' had to be introduced to the members' council, to join up with the various other parts of the club. This meant that every time a position on the council became free, we had to see whether an ex-footballer with a specific knowledge of a particular portfolio was available. If he wasn't, then a specialist could still be appointed. I didn't care that people were shaken up by my criticisms. As a top-level sportsman I'm used to criticism, because criticism is intended to make you better. That's how it works in top-level sport, so it must also apply to a top-level club.

By chance, Lucky Ajax, the association of ex-players, had a meeting around the time we were implementing these changes, so I was able to talk to everyone very effectively. The great thing was that from the most famous to the less well-known ex-players, everyone was prepared to help, and in the end seven former players were elected to the members' council. However, this was just the tip of the iceberg, because we also had to make use of all the knowhow that Ajax had at its disposal, by which I mean four generations of footballers in their thirties, forties, fifties and sixties, who all wanted to do what they could to help support their old club. Out of these ex-players could be formed a group that could stand by the administration and the directors when decisions had to be made. But first of all everything inside and around Ajax had to be thoroughly analysed to reach the right decisions, since, while we were busy discussing the future, a lot was going on behind the scenes to make sure everyone paid attention to football, because the first eleven had to go on performing.

While it had been my article that had started the discussions about how to overhaul the administration of the club, it was a joint effort between all of the ex-players involved. Of course, I was seen as a leader, someone who always ensured that the right people ended up in the right place on the team. This was the role I'd had throughout my career. I was the person who had taught that if a footballer didn't come into his own as a right-winger he might be an excellent right back. I wasn't the only one who benefited from that, the whole team did, and it was only natural that people saw me as a leader. This meant that I was heavily involved in the process of reshaping the Ajax administration. When we succeeded in getting through our proposals in the members' council election people said that I had won, but that wasn't how it felt to me. It was about Ajax, so the result was good for the club. It wasn't Cruyff who had won, it was Ajax, and this is how the new circumstances at the club ought to have been viewed, not with the focus on me.

First of all, everyone inside the club should have been proud that so many former players wanted to contribute to the future of Ajax. Particularly because those people brought a lot of quality to every aspect of the administrative team. They all wanted to work together to bring their club back up to the level where it needed to be. Not for themselves, but for Ajax, and the board of directors should have known that anyone fortunate enough to have been handed that much footballing knowhow on a plate should just make use of it, otherwise it is a complete waste of the talent and knowledge of the ex-players involved. In fact, though, we had not won, and the changes we made only widened the divide that was being created between me and the club. Because, as it happens, sadly, not everyone embraced progress, and one faction of the club remained opposed to the new development because they, it seemed to me, put their own self-interest first and feared that their role would be marginalized.

As a result, very soon after the council elections, there was an attempt from within the club to split the footballing bloc. There is a code of honour among footballers that you never abandon colleagues you've shared a changing room with, but during the reorganization of the club that also created an enormous emotional problem. In the new organization there seemed to be no room for one of our former colleagues, Danny Blind, who had played for Ajax for thirteen years from 1986–99, so knew everything there was to know about the club. And that was the decision everyone had to think hardest about. It is like a coach having to tell a loyal and valued player that there's no longer any room for him in the squad. Not because he's not a great guy or a good footballer, but because you want to go in a different direction in future. As a coach, those were always my most difficult moments, and I was very familiar with the situation we were having to go through at the club.

I saw first-hand, after the elections, how almost everyone wrestled with the fact that in Ajax's new approach there was going to be no room for Blind, and we were told that Danny was going to be let go. I was furious. I had brought Blind in as a defender and he was a terrific leader in the team and very intelligent, but when we tried to reason that Danny was a club icon, the issue was simply brushed aside.

Next we had to deal with the appointment of a new

board of commissioners. Three of the five board members were new to Ajax and had no direct connection with the club. So once again we had a board of whom the majority were without a club background. Despite this, I still had a feeling that, for all the club's administrative faults, there was a new readiness to make the most of everyone's know-how. One idea was that I would assess technical matters and present my findings to the new directors. My vision was primarily from the perspective of a footballer, and started with the composition of the squad. As a coach you choose an assistant who's different from you, just as you also appoint people you know have a better command of certain areas, and you delegate your responsibilities. Technical knowledge was my forte as both player and manager, so it made sense for me to be involved in choosing the person who would oversee the technical matters of the club. As I see it, that's also how you should deal with a board of commissioners. You don't let the fitness coach make decisions about scouting, so how can you let someone vote on an area that they don't know anything about?

On 11 February 2011, for the sake of the interests of Ajax, I took my place on the board of commissioners and became a member of one of the club's three 'sounding board groups'. After I had presented my plans to reform the club, in particular to rejuvenate the youth academy, the Ajax board of advisors and the CEO resigned on 30 March 2011. On 6 June 2011 I was appointed to the new Ajax board of advisors to implement my reform plans. But from day one I had a weird feeling about it. According to the rules I had to keep my mouth shut where the outside world was concerned. If I saw that something was going wrong, I wasn't allowed to say anything publicly without majority backing, even if it was about something I knew more about than the other commissioners, and something I'd ultimately be taking responsibility for if it didn't go to plan.

Was it in the interests of Ajax for me to stick to the rules, or should I speak out? The more I thought about the rules of the board of commissioners the more I came to the conclusion that I had to make my own rules. It's like the law: legislation doesn't protect you, it's there to deal with the offender. If you get beaten, then yes, someone gets punished, but you're still the one with the bruises. For me it was very simple – whatever the rules and regulations, the interests of my club outweighed everything else.

Unfortunately, almost as soon as I joined the board I ended up in the middle of a big political game. There were three candidates I thought we should consider for the new general directorship: Marco van Basten, Marc Overmars and Tscheu La Ling. These were three former players, three ex-internationals, all of whom had played for big foreign clubs and each of whom had his own special qualities. Marco was my first choice, but he had no interest because, having resigned as manager in 2009, he didn't yet want to return. I was later told by the interim board that Overmars and Ling didn't want to stand either. That was the last I heard of it until, by chance, I got talking to Tscheu La Ling and discovered that he hadn't even been approached. From that moment I was on my guard again and it soon became clear that my suspicions had been warranted. According to Ling, he had had a bad feeling about the decision that would be made after his first discussion with the other commissioners. In his view they didn't actually want a director, but a one-tier board. This was a set-up that I'd never heard of, but according to Tscheu it was an English management model in which the commissioners were also executives and were paid a salary.

He turned out to be right, and after that it went from bad to worse. As a member of the board of commissioners I tabled several questions about how Ling had been treated, but never received a straight answer. At the same time all kinds of stories about Tscheu appeared in the media, in which he was blackened by all sides. Both Tscheu and I had the unsettling feeling that all this was coming from someone closely involved with the board of commissioners. Nothing ever came of the accusations against Tscheu, but that didn't stop them being made. Whoever was talking to the press carried on doing so, and it became increasingly clear that these people were prepared to go a very long distance to have their way. At the same time, it turned out that Steven ten Have, who was on both the board of *De Tele-graaf* and the board of commissioners at Ajax, had pressed for my weekly column to be spiked, even though it was against the rules for a member of the board to get involved in the business activities of other commissioners. By now the atmosphere was so toxic that Ling decided to pull out, not least because van Basten seemed to have had a change of heart, and had told me that he was willing to assume the directorship. I was really happy about that, but things were soon to change.

After introducing Marco to ten Have, I had a commitment to go to an annual golf tournament at St Andrews. I told Marco he could discuss future plans with the football lads in the meantime, only to discover a few days later in St Andrews that he had reached an agreement with the board of commissioners, and that it was about to be presented. When I realized that Marco still hadn't talked to anyone on the football side of things, I put my foot on the brake. I made it clear that it was essential that there should be a collaborative approach to technical matters, to which everyone would contribute something from his own personal skill set. This is the type of thing you have to sort out in advance, not in retrospect. How can you reach an agreement with someone who has to fulfil a mostly technical role, when he hasn't had contact with the people who are going to have to carry out his plans?

Before I had gone to St Andrews we'd also agreed with all the training staff that they had to set a good example, and there must be no conflict of interest, or anything that looked like it. In that respect the situation at Ajax had got completely out of hand. I found out by chance that van Basten was involved in setting up a football-related business. Marco was listed as director and it turned out that he'd told ten Have about it, but he hadn't told me. I think Marco must have underestimated how important this was to me. He should have known that relations between me and the board of commissioners were critical, and in a situation like that you mustn't make it seem that you're one of them rather than one of us. How essential that last aspect was would become clear a week after Marco withdrew from the process. It started with a members' meeting in which ten Have said terrible things about Ling.

It was my turn next. During an edition of *Studio Voetbal* on NOS in November 2011, I was accused of racism because of remarks that I was supposed to have made to my fellow commissioner Edgar Davids. You're nearly sixty-five, you've been all over the world, and something like that is dumped on your plate. Let me explain it one more time. Ajax had been a multicultural club for years, but it had been

With his children - Susila, Jordi and Chantal - in Spain, 1981.

In 1985 Cruyff rejoined Ajax as coach. 'Sometimes I just sat on a ball by the side of the field and watched. There were people who said I was lazy. That's as may be, but if I'm sitting still I see more than if I move round. Sitting like that, I can analyse someone better, and see the details more clearly. Often details that 99 per cent of people don't know, don't see or don't understand.'

In 1987 Cruyff followed in the footsteps of his mentor Rinus Michels and won his first international trophy as manager of Ajax – the European Cup Winners Cup, a 1-0 win over Lokomotive Leipzig of East Germany.

Cruyff pictured with his son Jordi, in 1988, minutes after he had resigned as coach of Ajax. His time at Ajax established the football philosophy that his name has become synonymous with.

In 1988 Cruyff, seen here with President Núñez, joined Barcelona FC as manager. Between 1991 and 1994 Cruyff's 'Dream Team', including a young Pep Guardiola, won La Liga four times and won the European Cup Winner's Cup in 1989, and European Cup Final in 1992.

Cruyff celebrates winning the La Liga with Ronald Koeman in May 1993.

A young Jordi Cruyff played under his father at Barcelona before Cruyff was sacked in 1996 and Jordi moved to Manchester United to play under Sir Alex Ferguson.

In 1991 Cruyff underwent heart surgery and quit a lifetime's habit of smoking, replacing cigarettes with lollipops. He later said that 'football has given me everything in life, tobacco almost took it all away'.

Pictured with Leo Beenhakker and Louis van Gaal (below in the foreground). Cruyff's involvement with the leadership and management of Ajax FC after retiring from coaching was never far from the front pages.

The Cruyff Foundation, set up to give disabled and disadvantaged children a chance to play sport, was Cruyff's driving passion after stepping back from football.

Dennis Bergkamp, Johan Cruyff and Wim Jonk, all ex-players of Ajax, at the Amsterdam ArenA, 30 March 2011. The board of directors of Ajax resigned during a special meeting of the member council of the soccer club from Amsterdam because of a conflict between the club management and Cruyff.

In March 2016 Johan Cruyff passed away after a short battle with lung cancer. The friendly match between Holland and France, played a few days later, was paused at the fourteenth minute to mark his passing.

noticed that a lot of talented players from immigrant backgrounds dropped out around puberty. One of the reasons for involving Davids, who was born in Suriname, as a commissioner was to get a better understanding of this process. During a heated discussion I addressed him about his role on the board. Knowing me, I probably made no bones about it, just as I always did as a footballer and a trainer, because that's how it works in top-level sport. You always speak your mind, certainly in a one-on-one conversation, and I was probably quite direct. The comments I made had nothing to do with the colour of his skin and everything to do with his job as a commissioner. However, the most irritating thing was that the chairman of the board of commissioners, whom I'd been with at the members' council only a few hours earlier, called during the TV programme to confirm the racism story. He didn't tell me this, even though in another room the cameras were ready to record an interview by Edgar. All this was happening almost four months after Davids and I had disagreed, although the board of commissioners had met a number of times in the interim and the matter had never been mentioned. If there had been any genuine accusations of discrimination, any chairman worth a damn would have resolved the problem before the next board meeting, not leave it four months before revisiting the issue.

There was something else, too. When I was invited on to the board of commissioners, I'd always been aware that I couldn't write anything in my newspaper column about Ajax policy or internal club matters. So it was strange that the man who'd told me this phoned me up after the NOS programme to confirm the accuracy or otherwise of something that was supposed to have happened inside the board of commissioners. It was incredible to see how far removed certain people were from the fundamentals of what the club stood for. The worst thing for me was the way they looked down in a particular way on footballers who had played at the very highest level, but this is how they had treated Danny Blind, so I should have expected it.

During years of mismanagement, Ajax had lost a huge amount of money and made an awful lot of mistakes, but the same people who had that on their conscience were still trying to get their hands on whatever they could, meanwhile allowing people like me and Ling to suffer serious damage. Even though I'm used to this sort of thing, this was worse than anything I'd experienced before.

A few days later, at the end of 2011, the news broke that Louis van Gaal had been appointed to the general directorship. I didn't know anything about it, even though as a commissioner I should have been informed. The chairman replied that I'd been impossible to reach or hadn't responded to his calls, but none of it made any sense. The way Ling and I had had our names blackened, the denigrating attitude towards the footballers during the members' meeting and the procedure around the appointment of van Gaal were clear signals about how, in my view, the players, and thus the club itself, had been shafted, and to me it seemed that I had deliberately not been consulted. We considered that, in appointing van Gaal, the board had acted illegally, so the former players in the Ajax administration decided to instigate legal proceedings against the four commissioners as a collective, citing the board of commissioners rather than Ajax as a club. We wanted to give a clear sign that sportsmen would no longer be trampled over, and the fact that the younger generation of Ajacieds were willing to join in just reinforced me in my battle against the injustice I felt was done to the club by the commissioners. I was even more convinced that my generation had to take a step backwards, to act as background advisors for a new and ambitious group of former footballers whose mission was to bring Ajax back to the top of the European game.

The decision to take legal action was nothing personal against van Gaal and everything to do with the way the club was being run. Van Gaal and I were men in their sixties who needed to offer our experience to this new generation, but it was up to them whether they wanted to make use of it. It didn't have to be the case that older people like van Gaal and me grabbed the reins and joined the board. I had always been very clear that that wasn't good for anyone, and it didn't need to happen. In clubs around Europe younger ex-footballers were taking control. From the start my plan had been to make Ajax the trend-setter in Holland in that respect, and I wanted to turn Ajax into the first sports organization run by the sportsmen – this was part of the 'Cruyff Plan', with me on the sidelines as a proud spectator. But all our good intentions were undermined. The fact that we kept on believing in our mission was apparent in our collective decision to take legal action. Because we weren't the only ones who felt they had been mucked about to an extraordinary extent; the club and the supporters felt they had too. When great Ajacieds like Edwin van der Sar, Dennis Bergkamp, Ronald de Boer, Bryan Roy, Wim Jonk, Marc Overmars and many others stood up for the club, I thought it was actually the biggest compliment that Ajax could be paid.

After all the attention we got for taking the board of commissioners to court, we were going to have to wait two months for the judge's verdict. By now – in consultation with Louis van Gaal – Martin Sturkenboom and Danny Blind had been appointed as new directors, but because our technical plans had been rolled out by now, those appointments would cause enormous problems, because they just didn't fit with the plans that we had for the club.

Our first step when we had begun implementing the new structure had been to get rid of the job of technical director, because that's never worked at Ajax and never will. So the decision was made to replace it with a technical heart – a team comprising two ex-players and the head coach. The ex-players were Wim Jonk and Dennis Bergkamp, who between them had played at Inter, Arsenal, Ajax and PSV, so knew what it was like to be part of big, international clubs. If one of the areas of activity involved the first team then Frank de Boer, who took over coaching the first team in December 2010 after working with the youth teams since retiring from playing in 2006, also contributed to the decision making. This technical heart thus bore responsibility for everything to do with football inside the club. It all worked in theory, but the whole plan was undermined by the board of commissioners' action, and highlighted Ajax's greatest problem: a lack of trust. The appointment of van Gaal as a general director had made the situation inside the club worse than ever. Things became more insane by the day and suddenly all kinds of people started going on about how I had to get round the table with van Gaal, and that we'd sort things out after a good discussion. This ignored the way Sturkenboom and Blind had gone into action immediately after their appointment.

Without having read our technical plan setting out

the working of the technical heart, Sturkenboom decided to fire a colleague working under Jonk, and to give Jonk a written warning. Setting such a tone out of nowhere made me think that Sturkenboom had started a big clear-out as part of a completely different policy. Even more unsettling was the role of some in the administration outside the board of commissioners. While the supporters, trainers and footballers had clearly distanced themselves from the commissioners, the board of commissioners turned out to be in a position to bring two legal cases against Ling and the players' collective, at Ajax's expense. If someone deliberately tried to bring the club's most famous son into disrepute by identifying him as a racist, under normal circumstances he would be kicked out of Ajax straight away. But not our chairman, who then went on to say the most terrible things about Ling.

At the heart of this chaos was a struggle for the standards and values of Ajax. As I saw it, these were the standards and values that Ajax should uphold, but which had been trampled underfoot by the board of commissioners. To me it was curious that anyone who didn't uphold these standards wasn't immediately shown the door, but the board had the club in a kind of stranglehold. At that point the real Ajax had actually lost all power.

Incredible, but true. In particular Hennie Henrichs, the chairman of the board, tried several times to get me and van Gaal to work together. He sounded out both of us, although I later heard that he had been advised against this in all sections within Ajax. I wasn't at all surprised. Like many other Ajacieds, I didn't understand van Gaal's action in accepting the position of general director. Couldn't he see what was going on in the club, and that by taking this step he was running an enormous risk?

Some people claim that he was trying to take revenge on me in this way. But what for? The story goes that we'd had a row. The reason? I was said to have been angry because he hadn't thanked me properly before leaving a Christmas meal with my family, despite the fact he'd only left abruptly because his sister had died. I don't usually react to stories like that, but this time my family's moral standards were being questioned. If I were the type to become angry in such a situation, it wouldn't say much for me as a human being. It simply wasn't true.

What really happened was this. When van Gaal was an assistant trainer with Ajax and I was chief coach of Barcelona, he took a coaching course with me between Christmas and New Year 1989. Because my wife Danny didn't like the idea of a colleague sitting on his own in a hotel room during the festive season, she invited him to eat at ours. It was so convivial that we told him our door was always open to him during his stay. He came back the following day, but Danny and I had to go to a party, leaving van Gaal behind with my son Jordi and my friend Rolf. The three of them had a great evening. Pizzas were ordered, there was a bit of drinking and a lot of talk about football. He came back on the third evening, and while we were having a drink he suddenly received a phone call saying that his sister was ill. The next day he went back to Holland. We met up in the Netherlands again shortly afterwards and van Gaal was very friendly. He got on very well with my wife, who had met him in England in 1996 during the Euros. He told everyone she was the best hostess in the world, so it's not true that I, or anyone in my family, was angry because he had to leave without saying thank you.

I also think that it's strange that he never explained why he allowed himself to be used by the Ajax board of commissioners back then. After two months, in January 2012, the judge announced his verdict that the appointments of van Gaal, and subsequently of Sturkenboom and Blind, were illegal. Unfortunately, that didn't solve the problem. The commissioners simply ignored the ruling. That created the crazy situation whereby Ajax, which paid for the commissioners' defence team, now had to hire their own lawyers to get rid of the commissioners. In spite of the club's resignation demand, backed by a 73 per cent majority of Ajax shareholders, the commissioners refused, making all kinds of attempts to thwart the process of recruiting new members. All this after the commissioners had illegally appointed a director who didn't do what had been agreed with the club's technical directors. Right up to the end they were trying to govern from the grave by appointing their own successors, even though it was clear to see that they had no aptitude whatsoever for running a football club. However, finally they agreed that the board would be dismantled one commissioner at a time. I didn't trust that process so, as a commissioner, I agreed, but stipulated that I would be the last to go, to ensure that everything went according to plan.

Finally, in 2012, almost two years after I had set off the bomb in the wake of the disastrous match against Real Madrid, the new chapter could finally be opened. The whole fuss with the board of commissioners had made it clear that it wasn't just football that was going wrong for Ajax. The other thing that didn't add up was that the footballing side of the club was a majority shareholder in the publicly listed AFC Ajax NV, it had no say in how it governed itself and the directors and commissioners were really in a position to cut everyone else out of the decision-making process.

It isn't the managing director who's the most important part of the club, it's the first eleven. If the team performs well then it earns money, training is working and everyone's contented. Every facet of the club must be supportive of the first eleven. Whether you're a trainer or a steward, a director or a groundsman, a commissioner or a laundry-worker, you're Ajax. Everyone works in such a way so as to be of service to the first eleven. That way everyone is indispensable because of the part he or she plays, and the result is one club and one Ajax. If you haven't got that sort of mindset, you shouldn't bother involving yourself in the business of football. Of course, the playing squad hogs the limelight while the administrators wait in the wings, but these principles apply to all sections of a club, and the tasks of a members' council and a board of directors have to be fulfilled in a similarly team-oriented spirit. Youth training, for example, must be done by people who first and foremost have an understanding of football, but they must also have a back-up team with good skills in other areas, such as health, education and welfare.

In the two years that we had wasted sorting out the administration of the club, Frank de Boer had gone on performing, and had twice won the national championship with the first team. He had had a fantastic start as a trainer after his success with the youth team, and the current squad were showing great potential. For that reason, the Ajax board had a moral duty to ensure that he didn't get drowned in bureaucracy, as his predecessors had done, and was allowed to get on with his job. It was all too obvious that, in the past, because the organization of the club wasn't working, whoever was the first team coach always found himself running into a brick wall. We didn't want that to happen to Frank. The success of de Boer and his players had to be the start of a long period in which Ajax would become established at the highest level. That said, the reality was that, while they might have been successful in the league, the quality of the football they were playing was variable, and it was clear that there was still a long way to go to reach our shared goal. Unfortunately, success tends to overshadow well-intentioned criticism.

True to my word, I'd been the last commissioner to step down from the board. I now had no official position at Ajax, but it didn't keep me awake at night. All that fuss of the past two years had brought about a considerable change in me. According to Danny, I'd spent more time on the phone in one year than I had in the previous twenty, on top of which there was all that flying back and forth between Spain and Holland, which I paid for out of my own pocket. But I had been willing to do it because I was completely convinced that if I lost the fight, Ajax would be finished as a top-level club.

Michael Kinsbergen was appointed CEO of Ajax in November 2012. His mother was a friend of Danny's and I'd known Michael since he was a boy, so I was glad that the new board of commissioners had chosen him, because he was clearly the best man for the job. During his tenure, he brought in sports broadcaster Ziggo as the club's main sponsor for a record amount in Holland. He was also a good mentor to Edwin van der Sar, who had rejoined Ajax after six excellent years at Manchester United. Van der Sar had been appointed commercial manager, and he did an excellent job for the club. I also found it important that Michael was really busy pushing Edwin forward as a figure-head, while he himself stayed in the background. To me, that was a sign that the club's interests took precedence over his ego.

The one fly in the ointment was that because of the rules of the Amsterdam stock exchange, where Ajax was listed, Michael needed to depart from the original plan that we had drawn up for a three-member technical heart of the club to get the first team playing attractive football again. Because of the stock exchange rules, the technical heart had to include a director, so Marc Overmars was added as a fourth member to the triumvirate of Jonk, Bergkamp and de Boer, and appointed to the board as director of football.

A director of football is significantly different from a technical director. From now on Overmars was the person in charge of buying and selling players, and was formally responsible for scouting, medical personnel and everything that could directly influence 'football'. Of course, he had to discuss everything with Wim, Dennis and Frank, with each of them having his own internal responsibilities, but he was in charge overall, which had not been part of our original plan. It was also agreed that, while theoretically there might have been a hierarchy within this structure, in practice everyone worked on an equal basis. From the board of commissioners and the board of directors the former players Theo van Duivenbode, Dick Schoenaker and the former manager Tonny Bruins Slot were to remain available as advisors and keep a watchful eye open. With the management qualities brought by former minister Hans Wijers as the new chairman of the board of commissioners, and former KLM president Leo van Wijk, as one of the new commissioners, I had a good feeling about the fresh start we were making with Ajax.

Unfortunately, it didn't go as I had hoped. In the new organizational structure my role as advisor was meaningless, since I had no influence and there was nothing that I could formally contribute. As a result, I was unable to turn things round when they started going wrong again. Meanwhile, certain people were positioning themselves strategically in order to promote their own causes. While what I think is: you're in this spot, you have certain qualities, use those qualities to get everything in order for everyone. In my life in management I have always spoken my mind, and talked to my staff about what needed to happen before deciding what everyone had to do. Now I couldn't do any of that.

By contrast, after the reorganization at Barcelona,

which had been going on five years earlier under Frank Rijkaard, there was a clearer understanding straight away. When things were going well they phoned me up less often than they did when they weren't. That's how it should be. All it needs is a phone call if there's something that needs sorting out. But at Ajax, all they seemed to do was hold meetings. From almost the moment I took on the advisory role there I barely heard anything from the management, although, even from a distance, I did see differences of opinion cropping up about how my role should be used.

Of course, Barcelona had Rijkaard, whose footballing methodology and managerial experience were both great advantages. And then there was Guardiola, who took over the Barcelona first team in 2008. I'd trained both of them in a way, while among that generation of footballers at Ajax no one had been trained up by me. Even in the field of tactics they were educated in a country that doesn't actually count from a tactical point of view: van der Sar in England, Overmars in England; it's all English. And the English have never been that keen on tactics, so you couldn't have expected them to take my tactical message on board. All of which meant that in terms of football, what was going on at Ajax didn't have much to do with my vision of the game.

There were also other aspects that were out of kilter with what we'd included in the Cruyff Plan, which was a new technical vision for Ajax that my name was linked to. In reality there was no Cruyff Plan because my vision had been informed by the experiences that I'd acquired under experts like Rinus Michels and Jany van der Veen, and ideas that I'd accumulated as a trainer. For Ajax to succeed, first the foundations had to be sound, which would put the club as a whole in a better position to shift gear as improvements were made. But in my view Ajax failed to implement the basic principles of top-level football, so any plan, Cruyff or otherwise, was doomed from birth.

When I started out under Michels, during preparation for a competition we played a match every day rather than doing extra training. The intention was to be able to analyse as many situations as possible and at the same time increase our match fitness. By following that clear but simple procedure Ajax delivered dozens of world-class footballers, and that is why I've always worked according to similar basic principles. Like Michels, I believed in more matches rather than more drill sessions, but matches geared towards improvement. For example, at Barcelona I put the goalkeeper Andoni Zubizarreta in midfield on the left to let him get a lot of ball contact with his feet. That way I hoped to improve his connection with the rest of the team. The modern Ajax would never have dreamed of doing something like that.

These were the house rules that Ajax as a great European club was built on, and now the legacy of success was simply being ignored. By the way, this isn't an attack on Frank de Boer, who was nearing the end of his contract and who had faced all kinds of obstacles on the way.

Michael Kinsbergen was told, in 2015, that he had failed to give adequate leadership to the club, after which his contract wasn't extended. I thought that was unfair. He had not only concluded the best sponsorship deals in the history of the club, but also redefined van der Sar's position in the club in such a way that he was now a great asset to Ajax. Kinsbergen was being unfairly blamed for, among other things, the tensions in the technical heart between Jonk on one side and Bergkamp and Overmars on the other. I didn't understand much of it, but such things happen, and Kinsbergen had to deal with it as best he could. In my view, Theo van Duivenbode especially, as a commissioner with a top-level football background, should have made his voice heard more clearly. Instead, I was forced to ask the board to bring in the pragmatic Tscheu La Ling to undertake an in-depth analysis of the club's situation and try to resolve what was clearly a deep-seated problem.

I wasn't alone in my concerns. There were calls for me to be more closely involved in the running of the club again, but that would have proved impossible from a practical point of view, because I live abroad and would have had to be away three or four days a week. Anyway, that had never been what I'd set out to do. The principle I had always adhered to as part of the Ajax administration was to try to create a few basic conditions that would provide the best for those in charge, and after that it was up to the new generation of Ajacieds to shape the future of the club on the basis of a shared vision. I have always said that it's essential that another generation should carry that out. I knew that even I don't have eternal life, and I was already having problems with my health.

Ling's report, which was leaked at the end of 2015, revealed that the fundamental qualities of the former players involved were excellent, but he also discovered shortcomings that the players couldn't do much about because they lacked the experience even to define the problem, much less correct it. The best that they could do was acknowledge that they sometimes needed help. This hadn't been available in the past, but now, on the basis of Ling's report, extra avenues of assistance were created.

Although Tscheu had written an excellent report, it quickly became apparent that some of those involved thought everything was just fine. Doubts were cast once more on his input and his character. Unfortunately, this time it came from Ajax itself rather than just individual administrators. The aggravating thing was that unfair criticism of Ling was used by some as an excuse to carry on as before. Meanwhile, Ling had prevented the former players in the organization from being sacked en masse. The board of commissioners was completely at odds with one particular individual and didn't want to extend the contracts of others. Tscheu bowed to that because he wanted to start his investigation with a clean slate, but he saved the jobs of many. That makes the way some of the former players reacted to him, both in private and even publicly, all the more unpleasant.

This kind of thing took a lot of the fun out of watching and supporting the club. Not least because the football itself was becoming less and less attractive, and as a spectator I was getting bored. The players were spending far too much time retreating rather than pressing the ball while, in possession, there was far too much lateral play. The build-up play was sometimes so sluggish that midfielders and forwards ended up bunched together.

Clearly, something needed to be done, but before splashing out fortunes on new players it first had to be established whether the present squad were playing to their full potential. This should have been the job of the technical heart, but I kept hearing about strengthening the squad and the return of old hands, with no clarity on whether everything had been done within the club to deal with the fundamental technical problems they had. This didn't just mean improving training, but also a better scouting system and closer collaboration with affiliated clubs like Ajax Cape Town and AS Trenčín.

The embarrassing thing was that, by the end of 2015, only one team at Ajax was playing in a way that was close to my vision: Wim Jonk's A1, the first junior squad. It was clear that the football problem at Ajax was a consequence of bad technical policy. I talked to the players about passing and taking the ball, control, positional play, performance, but it was too much for them to absorb. I was sure that our defensive set-up, and the way we built up and shifted gear, just had to change. Lateral passes and intersecting lines, meaning that there was no space between the players, wasn't our football. We had to find, as quickly as possible, a new on-field blueprint. The way we were playing at the moment was boring, didn't bring results and was wrecking our talented players. The public wasn't having it.

Better training was necessary to produce the kind of skilful and entertaining football that Ajax was always associated with. We all needed to work on that by keeping the peace in the club and closely monitoring the development of everyone involved, determining who can do even better and who needs to operate in a different way. And everyone had to remember that everything they did had to be in the best interests of Ajax.

Meanwhile, I was also having more and more doubts about the intentions of commissioner Leo van Wijk. On 11 September 2015, before the report was leaked, van Wijk, Ling and I had gone through the whole of it together. Leo had enthusiastically agreed with every word of the report, which was why, four days later, Tscheu and I were dumbfounded when the board took measures which were more or less the opposite of what we had discussed with van Wijk. For example, van der Sar had urged for Kinsbergen to be brought back, because he was now so busy that he hardly had a personal life any more. Instead, Edwin was given even more to do, promoted from commercial manager to marketing director and at the same time told he had to run the technical heart of the club. Meanwhile, Overmars was moved from director of football to players' director, with *sole* responsibility for the buying and selling of players and the drawing up of contracts, a position that requires a lot of caution because if what needs to be done is explained badly, misunderstandings can easily occur. The last year's signings were indicative of that. Too often Jonk's voice, as an expert on his own talented trainees, was unheard when a player was transferred. Dolf Collee was also appointed general director. He had been a banker, but he too had just let the specialists get on with things for years as a commissioner. At first I hoped that he would at any rate be able to hold things together, and that he would be supportive of the former players. But very soon the opposite proved to be the case.

By early November 2015 I'd had enough. For years I'd known that the core of my vision for Ajax was being ignored. I suspected this was deliberate, and I don't play games like that. Eventually, the pragmatist in you comes to the conclusion that it's pointless trying to add something when you're getting absolutely nothing in return. At my age I don't need badges or medals any more. It's incredibly sad that, at the age of sixteen, I was there for the beginning of the ascendancy, and now, at nearly seventy, I have to witness the decline. No one wants to listen. Or rather, hardly anyone wants to listen. Everyone has his own agenda. If the problem had been confined to Ajax, it might arguably all have been my fault, but if you look at Dutch football as a whole, and the national side's failure to qualify for Euro 2016, you begin to wonder who on earth is doing what. We're all so busy beating ourselves on the chest, but if you look at the results you can reach only one conclusion, the journey we've taken has led to our demise, and that's very sad.

Two weeks after I left the club at the end of 2015, Collee fired Wim Jonk. So within six months the CEO and the head of training had both gone, and these were the very same people who had revived Ajax's finances. When Collee introduced himself to me, he immediately told me that he had absolutely no understanding of football. Tscheu and I told him we would help him with that side of things. Except he never called me. It is true that he sat down with Tscheu about three times, but nothing came of it. Even when Ling's report clearly showed where the problems lay, he didn't do anything with it.

Collee comes from ABN Amro, which means he's a banking man, someone who mightn't know anything about football, but must know something about numbers. Since Jonk came to the club about €85 million had been earned from selling players that we'd trained ourselves, his team was ahead of the competition and hadn't dropped a single point in the Champions League for youth teams. When the proof is on the table that the whole financial healing of Ajax is due largely to the collaboration between Jonk and de Boer, how can you throw 50 per cent of your formula for success out the door?

We saw another commissioner, Theo van Duivenbode, as one of us. As an ex-player himself, he should have been the key figure for the former players, but he pretty much went along with everything the board said. Take scouting, which was criticized because the first-team scouts and the people involved in training didn't work together and they weren't recommending good players. Yet the best scout there is, Tonny Bruins Slot, who I had worked with for eleven years, was on the board. If the coaches didn't ask for his help, at least van Duivenbode should have pointed out it was available to them. Perhaps some on the training staff might have felt too proud to ask a board member for advice, but surely the important thing is that if you use your quality, your standards rise and life gets easier for everyone. I can still remember a discussion I had with van Duivenbode after the board of commissioners had suggested we should buy a certain player. Theo said it involved an awful lot of money that we didn't have. Two weeks later the player was bought anyway, and van Duivenbode had been one of the signatories. Then I wondered to myself: What have you been doing for the last two weeks? Did you try to persuade people or not? If you think a player isn't worth the money and somebody else thinks otherwise, then you go to Bruins Slot and ask him, 'Look, should we pay that sum or not?'

Van Duivenbode became too involved and that's why things went wrong in the technical heart as well, and why Jonk was dismissed. I blame him for that. As a representative of the footballers on the highest management body I feel he should have been much more protective of the youngsters.

Unfortunately, no one could see that Ajax had to escape the situation of being run by people who have ended up in football but actually know almost nothing about it. They couldn't see that the item at the top of the agenda should have been how Ajax could become Ajax again. Perhaps by buying up all the shares or leaving the stock exchange or whatever, as long as we come back to our own club culture. By now I've had dealings with two boards of commissioners, and my experiences are overwhelmingly negative. Above all, I feel I was misled to a huge extent by the two chairmen.

Of course, we all make mistakes. We've all tried our hand at something new, and inevitably some things don't go well straight away. The important thing is that you learn from your mistakes and help each other to do it better. But in this case, such cooperation was out of the question. The proof of that is right in front of our eyes, and I always felt that this was one of the reasons I was let go. The way the board went about their business produced negative energy that doesn't suit football. Members and fans must be able to go to the stadium to enjoy themselves and support their club. Sadly, within Ajax there's still too much politics going on, at the expense of both football and the club.

Am I disappointed in the younger former players? Yes, although I think that has to do with the way they were trained, which has instilled in them a particular way of playing football, a particular way of looking at the game. That's why where you've played and who has managed you is so important, because that teaching informs the legacy that you will leave behind as well as allowing you to make the distinction between the best and the rest. Take, as an example, Bayern Munich. They were still playing in the second division about fifty years ago, but these days they're the standard bearers for quality football. By choosing directors and trainers who set certain standards on the field, they are the club that people are looking to to see the future of the game. They showed that the way to improve is not by copying what happens in Spain or Italy, but by looking first at yourself. And looking at yourself means determining your abilities and addressing your shortcomings. You can't demand that a German must play football like a Dutchman. Or an Italian. You just can't. So don't look at them. Sort yourself out first, that has always been my philosophy. Even the excuses for not doing so are predictable, and, of course, often revolve around money, but at the end of the day it's a match of eleven against eleven. Even the richest club can't put twelve men on the field. It's always a matter of basic qualities, and don't try to tell me that we don't have basic qualities in Holland these days, either at Ajax or in the national team. It is simply not the case that we had such skills for forty years and now all of a sudden we don't. That's madness, but it is a logical consequence of the fact that, during training, the players no longer learn what they need to develop.

Luckily, there are always exceptions like Wim Jonk, and that's why he's a friend of mine. When no one else in Ajax was performing, he was doing just that with his youth team, and getting them to work on technique. But even though his success was obvious, no one asked how he was achieving it, and rather than setting him up as a model, Jonk was moved to areas in which he had little experience. He told me about endless meetings he had to attend, knowing that they would lead nowhere. He was absolutely right about that, because football at Ajax isn't about meetings; it's about scoring goals, dominating the game and making sure that you make it into the next round, whichever way you do it. But too many people do the thinking at Ajax, which means that it's all about compromises and survival, and the skills required to dominate and win matches get completely lost.

This is precisely my point. Ajax actually consists of two clubs in one – professionals and amateurs – and the amateurs, who aren't supposed to have any power, are still able to fire the bosses of the professional club. So you get a huge amount of misplaced influence that has nothing to do with the game. Football consists of different specialisms, and every specialist has his own peculiarities, so within certain parameters you have to let specialists go their own way. You should never tell a specialist what to do. As for meetings, if you have something you want to talk about and you know in advance that it's three against one, why would you go? It's pointless. Far better to discuss the qualities of one player or another, how talent can be improved or shortcomings solved. Rather than holding meetings you should create something positive on both the individual and the team level. Then talking has a point.

Holland is a small country, so you have to be creative and keep your eyes open for new talent in your immediate environment, but also in places where you can sign players before another club or a manager comes and takes them away. There are dozens of details that you all have to work on together. Sometimes it works, sometimes it doesn't, but you have to be in a position to recognize the possibilities in the first place.

That's why the things I'm saying about football now are the same things I was saying twenty years ago. I'm not changing my mind. But there's something else; something that's new and that I didn't know then. That people shouldn't just bring their own qualities, but should be ready to share knowledge with or learn from others. I've applied the same philosophy to the Cruyff Institute. You've got students from the whole world sitting there, but when they're studying you've got to bring them all together. To create a strong collective from which the sport benefits in the end.

That was also my attitude when, after all the fuss, we were finally able to get to work at Ajax with the aim of growing towards the top of European football. That was realistic. When it comes to technique, tactics and performance I know what I'm talking about, because it worked for me in the eighties at Ajax and later at Barcelona too. With attractive football from a mixture of home-grown talent and a few star purchases the big prize was won within two years.

Again, look at Bayern Munich. They managed to do what no one thought they ever could: they bridged the gulf separating them from the top teams in Italy, Spain and England, and this from a club that is not even in its country's capital. But you will always be dependent on people with knowhow. Everything and everyone, whatever position they might occupy, must put his qualities at the service of the rest, and the rest must reciprocate.

Wim Jonk is a prime example. He's open to things, but they have to be done well. You can't just say to him, 'I don't agree with you, clear off.' You can't do that, because he's the best, so he has to be in charge. Of course, he'll make mistakes, but then they must be held up to the light to convince him that other people have ideas to contribute. The problem comes when someone who knows a lot is written off by someone who knows less. So many CEOs and directors think they have to control those below them, while in fact it should be precisely the reverse. They should allow themselves to be guided by those who know better. Their inflated egos urge them to lay down the law when they just don't have the knowledge to do so.

You can immediately identify such people when you ask them a question, whatever the field. Either you get an answer from someone who places himself in your shoes, or you get an answer from someone who tries to convince you he's right, and that his solution is the only solution. When I ask a question, I just want to know what I need to know, because, ultimately, information is more important than intelligence. I don't need chapter and verse; as long as I get the right answers from the right people, then I'm a step ahead of someone who might have more understanding but less information. That's why as a coach I assembled as big a team as possible to be responsible for all elements of training and preparation. It wasn't about being the boss and issuing tasks, it was about ensuring that other people who were better at something than I was were more easily able to do it. I had to create a situation whereby they could do that and not have me telling them what to do. The specialists I appointed weren't my assistants, but people in charge of a particular area, just as I was in charge of technique and tactics.

Unfortunately, few directors are sufficiently broad-minded to work like that. Often you see the urge to put themselves in the limelight while others do the work, and in all my years in football this is something I've never under-stood. As I've always said, you need to leave the experts to do their job. After all, if you've got toothache, you go to the dentist because he understands teeth. If suddenly you can't see very clearly, you go to the optician because he's the guy who knows about eyes. It should work in football exactly the same way. So if problem A comes up, you've got someone in the club who understands what causes problem A and can solve it. If you don't have that attitude as a boss or a manager, you'll be kept pretty busy.

It's the same with medical matters. Ajax had doctors, but what they needed was someone with a good medical contacts book. Someone who knew immediately how to deal with a particular problem, not by treating it himself but by knowing who could. Someone like that sends a footballer for treatment and then monitors the whole process that follows. He doesn't need to do the operation himself. His quality is that he knows who's best at solving the problem and arranging an appointment for the player, ensuring he ends up where his problem will find the best solution. But who of the commissioners, chairmen or whatever they're called, checks whether their doctor does that? Whether he's good at managing the players' health. That doesn't just apply to the medical personnel.

In that respect, Davy Klaassen, one of the current Ajax stars, and I tried to set a good example. He'd been injured for a while and couldn't play, but no one knew what was wrong with him. Then I brought in an acquaintance of mine from Barcelona to see if he could work out what the problem was. He immediately called up all kinds of specialists, even for eyes and teeth. Eventually, he found someone who said, 'Hey, that's my area, I understand that problem.' Suddenly Klaassen could be treated, and was able to play again shortly afterwards. So that's the idea, and that's how it should be. But it's only possible if you're prepared to swallow your pride and acknowledge that there are people who are better than you and that you've got them in your little black book.

An attitude like that also works with someone like Frank de Boer. He didn't get guidance, help or support from anyone, and that was why he clung too tightly to a vision that didn't speak to me or lots of the supporters. But in an organization that isn't able to get the best out of people, you'll find it tough even as a coach. My reference today is the style of play of Barcelona and Bayern, and I see too little of that at Ajax at the moment, which is ironic because those two clubs more than any others have been inspired by Ajax, and look how successful they have been. But if your own club no longer has the will or the vision to supply that, you just have to be honest and detach yourself from it.

I'm coming to the conclusion that it was a good decision to cut my ties with the club. Not least because of the way Ajax treated Wim Jonk and Tscheu La Ling, two people of whom I'm enormously proud. As head of training, Wim did demonstrably good work, and was then fired. He was the only one who carried out the essence of the Cruyff Plan; a man who wanted to talk about football, but had to leave because he wouldn't become part of the administration. Ling tried to help by attempting to make Ajax more a football club and less a business, but when I see how people reacted to his report, with all kinds of weird insinuations, it's very telling.

In the end, the time will surely come when the club realizes things need to change. If they work that out, there are enough people to make things come together as the truly committed members and supporters want them to, and when that happens I'll be part of that, because I'll always be there for Ajax. If a problem needs solving, health permitting, I'm always ready to be there, but only if everyone's behind me. Because I've now adopted a positive attitude – I assume that everything will turn out fine, and that the revolution we started all those years ago with Michels will prove to have been good for something. That we've had to take a few knocks along the way so that we can get ourselves together. It might take a year, ten years, who can say? At any rate, it'll happen when the right people start being listened to. People who hold the club in their hearts and who know what Ajax represents. If that happens, our struggle will not have been in vain.

12

I've done almost everything in football. As a player, as a coach and as a manager. The only thing missing is full-time national coaching. I think that's the only real failure in my career. As I've grown older I've been increasingly disgruntled that I was passed over by Rinus Michels in 1990 to coach the Dutch team during the World Cup. I patched things up with Michels, but it still leaves a sour taste that I wasn't able to do something very special, especially because the time was ripe. The international players were in the prime of their career and after winning the Euros in 1988 they were ready for the greatest success in Dutch footballing history. The same applied to me as coach and, given my history at club and national team level, I just expected I'd be appointed. It was even generally well known that both the players and I wanted that to happen, because it would have allowed us to bring our strengths together and finally become world champions, as we should have done in 1974 and 1978. But it didn't happen, because Michels had other ideas. Against the wishes of major internationals like Ruud Gullit, Marco van Basten, Frank Rijkaard and Ronald Koeman, he left me to one side.

As the technical board member, it turned out that he didn't want to stick his neck out within the KNVB, apparently because he had heard that I wanted to overthrow the whole organization. Codswallop. Of course, I wanted to assemble my own technical staff and backroom staff, so that we could put everything into our bid for the world title and give ourselves the best possible chance, but that wouldn't have meant overthrowing the KNVB. I'd pay with my head if we failed, so I simply wanted to stipulate the terms under which the team was chosen, which is what I had always done as a manager. In key positions I'd have people who were used to coaching at the highest level and under the greatest pressure every week, and not people who do something like that once every two years.

Michels and I talked it through later on. Immediately after the World Cup he came to our training camp in Barcelona to give me an explanation. The discussion was all very amicable, but I still don't understand what was behind his decision. Maybe it was jealousy, who knows. Of course, he's a guy who's been everywhere, and who's enjoyed great success wherever he's been, and that always strokes someone's ego. Perhaps hearing every day that I was actually really good, that he could have worked really well with that guy Cruyff, put him on the defensive.

I've found myself thinking that it wasn't surprising that Michels had heart problems, because he often had to pretend to be someone he wasn't. I know that, because I knew the man he really was. He was very tough, but, as I knew, if necessary he would take you to the doctor in person and give you a massage himself. He really cared. And if we were sitting in a restaurant or had a party, he would start singing in the middle of dinner, and I found myself thinking: How in the name of Christ can he do that, when he's just half-killed us in training?

When we were together at Los Angeles Aztecs in 1979 I discovered that he was superstitious. Once we won when

Michels was wearing a pair of very distinctive shoes – white ones with black tassels; the kind golfers wear. They looked awful, but he wore them on match days for a long time because he thought they brought good luck. He would never have done that in Europe, where he had a particular image, and I think he wanted to hang on to that. He sometimes had to force himself to maintain that image of himself. In that respect Michels was a man of extremes, who didn't make things easy for himself. Even though he cocked up the World Cup in 1990 for a great generation of footballers and for me, I still have a warm feeling towards him. He was there for me after my father died, when I sometimes found it hard to stand on my own feet, and I can't forget that.

That's happened to me often in my life – people I had a special bond with suddenly letting me down. Like with Michels, but also with Piet Keizer, Carles Rexach and later Marco van Basten. In retrospect, perhaps it was all very human. It's also something that happens with the greats, that all of a sudden there's a kind of competition, and because they're supposedly great, they decide to stop listening. Over the years, I've tried to put myself in their place, particularly with Michels, Keizer and Rexach. When I think about it, I've learned a lot from them all, but they've never been willing to learn from me. I think that's a very telling difference. Take Piet Keizer. When I first got to know him as a young lad he was three or four years older than me. I had no father, so he took me under his wing. 'Go home, pal, go and sleep, you've got a match tomorrow,' he would say to me. Then he probably went out on the town himself, but he was a guy who kept an eye on me. I was sixteen or seventeen and I sometimes pinched his motorbike or rode off on someone else's bicycle. At any rate I got up to all kinds of tricks, and when that happens it's good to have an older person to rein you in a bit. That's important, until the moment when something changes. Like the vote in the Ajax players' group when Piet was elected captain over me, which led me to move to Barcelona. And the way later on he didn't agree with me about the way I wanted to reorganize Ajax. But as I've said before, perhaps it's only human. At any rate I feel no rancour towards him. I still have my own thoughts on the matter, but I'll never forget the help I had from him.

The issue over Carles Rexach, who was my assistant coach at Barcelona until I got sacked, is more a question of mentality. Of course, Michels was stubborn and I'm probably stubborn as well, but Rexach wasn't. He never went against the grain, while if I did he often spoke his mind to me. When that happened he often went further than me. In the end I ascribed our differences to the fact that he possessed a Catalan mindset. Whether that came from his upbringing or his schooling, I don't know, but when it came down to it Rexach never connected at all with the Dutch mentality or my way of thinking. He gave me his opinion, but he himself never went into action. He couldn't keep up with that, while I've always been the kind of person who has something to say if things aren't working. And I have always made sure that I both speak my mind and offer a possible solution. At any rate, you would have had no doubts what I thought about things whereas Rexach went along with the flow – that was the key difference between the two of us.

Marco van Basten was an extremely good footballer, and very intelligent in all kinds of ways. He didn't necessarily need me or want to learn from me. That's different from how things worked with Pep Guardiola, for example. As a player at Barcelona they wanted to get rid of Pep because they thought he was a lanky great beanpole who couldn't defend, who had no strength and couldn't do anything in the air. So he was blamed for all the things he wasn't good at, while I thought they were all things he could learn to do well. What all those people didn't see was that Guardiola had the fundamental qualities needed for the top level: speed of action, technique, insight. Those are phenomena that very few people exhibit, but in his case they were present in spades. That's why I'm now following the development of Sergio Busquets with great interest. Everyone at Barcelona talks about everyone else, they're all so good. But I'll be interested to see them when Busquets is no longer in the squad. I think everyone will be shocked by the change it'll bring about. I also think Busquets is going to become a good coach. Like Guardiola, he is someone who's had to work extra hard to get to where he is. Success didn't come easily to either of them.

As well as his footballing qualities, Guardiola has a very strong personality and an intelligent mind. You can talk to him about any subject under the sun. He reads a lot, and was able to learn German very quickly when he joined Bayern Munich. People like that never have problems asking questions, and although Guardiola isn't the kind who would rely on my advice, he is curious to know what I think.

I still remember when he was appointed coach at Barcelona B. He wanted to know what I thought about it and I told him that in my view there was one rule he had to apply. He had to be able to say to the chairman: 'Bugger

off out of the changing room, I make the decisions here.'
Only then would he be fit to be coach of the first team. If
he didn't do that, he would have to stay with the second.
What I meant was that he had to be the boss, and the one
who decided what had to happen, with all the consequences
that brought. But never under any circumstances should he
let himself be fired because of someone else's initiatives.
You've got to be able to say in retrospect: 'I've been an idiot,
but I was responsible for what I did.' Or: 'I did this well and
I'll do it like that next time too. Whatever they say or do.'
Pep's thinking went quite a long way in that direction and
he picked things up and combined them with a vision of
his own.

Despite him also being highly intelligent, my relationship with van Basten has always worked differently. I
thought about it, and in the end I saw an essential difference
between Pep and Marco. As I've already said, without me at
Barcelona, Guardiola would very probably have been sold.
Van Basten's a completely different story. He'd have been a
world-class footballer even without me. He didn't really
need me for that. But he probably thought of me as the man
who put him on the field against FC Groningen early in his
career at Ajax, when his ankle was in a doubtful condition.
The match in which his injury became so aggravated that,
years later, he was forced to end his career prematurely. I've
tried to put myself in his position, and I've come to understand why it was that he didn't respect all my advice later
on. It was a kind of revenge for the time that he let me persuade him to play in the match that would overshadow the
rest of his career. If I think about it like that, his reaction is
entirely understandable. That's why I now see the problems
with Michels, Keizer, Rexach and van Basten as primarily

caused by the way we are. Our personalities. I don't hold a grudge against any of them. I sorted things out with Michels again before his death in 2005, and I'm back in touch with Piet as well.

I still give these matters a lot of thought, and I've drawn an incredible amount of positive energy from the reactions of former teammates and players I'd managed since I learned in October 2015 that I've got lung cancer. Even from those you could hardly say I'd treated with kid gloves. It does show a particular kind of respect because even though we've disagreed, they've all come to the conclusion that reconciliation was the only way forward. This has been a good thing for me to learn after all those years, because I've wondered how they would take it; whether they'd ever see it my way. I was always capable of putting things nicely, but sometimes I just couldn't.

At the top of football all of us were always under pressure, and every now and again we would reach breaking point. That's true in the changing room, but as soon as we were outside all the arguments were over, for me at least. It's good to see that as the players of those days have grown older they've also come to gain greater understanding, which means that instead of incomprehension there's respect. Sometimes it goes even further than that, and I discover that things I barely noticed, they found quite exceptional. Whether it's Ronald Koeman or one of the juniors, that kind of thing is extremely satisfying.

Of course, that applies very much to Guardiola's remark about what I brought to Barcelona: 'Johan built the cathedral, and it's up to us to maintain it.' That's not just a brilliant choice of words, but also very touching. Because I've simply done what I thought was best for everyone, both at Barcelona and at Ajax. Luckily, it worked at Barcelona, but it is mostly thanks to people like Frank Rijkaard, Henk ten Cate, Pep Guardiola and Txiki Begiristain that the cathedral, as Pep so beautifully called it, is still standing. I'm very grateful to them for that. Because this isn't just the football I love, it's the football the supporters love as well. It's football as football must be.

I feel positive about the future of football, although I think for now there will be a period of considerable chaos. What rules for the time being is money, which is something most obvious in England. Commerce is part of it, and it's good too, but everything has its place. In that respect it's not the footballers and the commerce that cause the problems, but mostly directors who won't leave the sporting side alone. Take the development of native English talent, which in turn has an influence on the national squad. You run a risk when too many foreign players are playing in the Premier League. One solution might be to limit foreign players to a maximum of five per matchday squad. To be absolutely clear, I have nothing against foreign players. Where that's concerned I was even a pioneer when I was brought to Barcelona. I added something that was missing from the team, just as Velibor Vasović and Horst Blankenburg were brought to Ajax when I was there.

Once I advised the Dutch football association to recommend a gentlemen's agreement among the professional clubs, with everyone promising to include at least six players with a Dutch passport in their starting eleven. This would force clubs to pay more attention to their youth training. Of course, a welfare policy is an excellent thing, but you have to look out for yourself as well. I don't mean that in a positive or a negative way, but completely object-ively, purely in the interest of football, where things are often different from other walks of life and have different effects. Forget for a moment the wider European picture and decide, as a Dutch collective, to bring all the domestic clubs together and agree to field at least six players with a Dutch passport, hence at most five without. I don't give a damn what they do in Spain and England; this is what we think, and we should look after ourselves first, just as the Americans did. No one there has disproportionate influ-ence on the policy of Major League Baseball, the NBA or NFL. They're organized in such a way that all decisions can be made in the interest of the sport. Where that's concerned, Europe is way out of date. Apart from that, home-based owners often no longer have the money. That comes from outside, which means that decisions affecting the domestic game are increasingly made from board-rooms in America, Asia and the Middle East. That creates a lack of balance, and it is essential that every country should think on the basis of its own situation. Otherwise, the whole thing goes even further out of kilter. Once upon a time clubs in Holland, Belgium and Scotland were part of setting the tone in top-level European competition, but today they no longer really count. Has their interest in the game fallen so far behind the rest, or have they just been outflanked, because they don't have enough money? This is an open question. It is much more important to ask what can be done about it.

Top-level football is about technique, tactics, training and finance, and it's been like that forever. Circumstances at a club or in a country can change, but the fundamentals remain. In the Netherlands, technique has always been the basis of football. You have to cling to that at all times since you can't play any other way, because the Dutch public won't accept it. It's the same in Catalonia. I hope it stays that way too, with trainers and coaches basing their choices on the squad. Iniesta and Xavi, for example, aren't 'two fast midfielders' but 'two footballers'. And a footballer has to have the ball at his feet. He has to run as little as possible, because the more tired he gets, the worse his technique will be. That's why you have to deal with the question of how you can limit the detrimental effects of running on a particular player. Which option do you choose? A higher level of fitness, better technique, more speed? The answer is that you go for the quality that will please the fans. Because you're playing for the public, after all. I can't turn up as a Dutchman in England or Italy and go and play football the way that pleases me. No, you play football the way the public wants you to. The public has to come to the stadium, and that stadium has to be full. You see that at Barcelona too, where they made their choice and have clung to the same vision for almost thirty years. The coach who wants to change that has a problem, because the public won't like it.

So the ethos is the same, but the big difference between Barça's Dream Team in the 1990s and Guardiola's team was agility. The question was not whether the club's vision should be changed but rather whether it could be made even better. So you had to keep on asking the question: should this be done faster? If it was something important, like keeping possession, then work on passing the ball more quickly without sacrificing accuracy. If it wasn't important, then don't worry about it. You've also got to be able to gauge what is fast and what isn't. The analysis of a detail in top-level football is the hardest thing of all. The ability to analyse the whole thing in such a way that you can grab victory not through the move itself, but sometimes two or three moves before. How is a ball received and how is it played on? Did it require one touch or two? How good was the receiving player's control? Then you also have to deal with the defender. Someone who plays in a good squad is inclined to relax a bit against weak teams. Then the tempo comes down and the balls don't arrive. Or arrive too late. It's details like that that you have to be able to see. This is now the problem in the Netherlands. The whole world still talks admiringly about our way of playing football, except that there are very few Dutch coaches who know how to train players to do it. I saw that was happening about fifteen years ago. Different choices in formation were being made, which meant space was being used in a different way.

When you eat, you use a knife and fork. It was like that a hundred years ago, and a hundred years from now it will still be the case. Some things just don't change. The same applies to football. First the basics have to be in place, and it's only then that you can make improvements. In the Netherlands the basics have been compromised. The food's prepared by the best cooks, but we're forgetting how to hold the knife and fork. One good example is the goal-keeper. When, in 1992, the rules changed so that keepers were no longer allowed to pick up the ball from a back pass, they were forced to improve their kicking technique. Until then, most keepers had very poor kicking technique, but these days 90 per cent of them have a better long-range passing than 90 per cent of outfield players. This proves that skill can be acquired through training. These days too, every goalie can work equally well on either foot. How come they can all do that yet only about a quarter of outfield players are two-footed? It shows that a goalkeeper knows that kicking with both feet is an essential skill that he has to work on, and that working on it pays off. Why don't outfield players do the same?

Team training sessions are all well and good, but players also need to understand how their individual skills can be improved for the benefit of the team. As a manager, do you give players homework to do? Or after a session do you take a couple of them aside and explain the difference between a pass through the air and one along the ground – that a ball that goes along the ground travels more slowly. It looks easier, but in practice it's harder to control effectively and requires just as much concentration from the receiver. That's why you often see poor control of a slow pass, because the receiver isn't concentrating properly, whereas if you play the ball hard concentration is usually greatest and the chance of mistakes reduced. At least two players are involved in any move, but too much attention is paid to how they play individually when it's really about how they play together.

Also, the physical and mental condition of players is always subordinate to football. Of course they both need to be considered, but always from the point of view of football. If someone is off form, start with their football before trying to analyse them mentally, because if the football is good there's so much positive energy generated that the mental and the physical sides might well cease to be a problem. Think back to when you were a child. When you played football after a full day at school, did you get tired? No. You just slept well that night.

Outside influences can also affect the way players perform on the pitch. Journalists are always looking for something to write in their papers, but as soon as you start to believe what you read in them you're in danger of fooling yourself. The only one whose opinion of you matters is your manager. Newspaper reports are written to sell newspapers. It's nice to read something positive and less nice if it's critical, but often the reporter's assessment deviates from your manager's. The two things need to remain clearly separate. Reports of Barcelona games almost always concentrate on Messi, Neymar and Suárez, but it's Iniesta and Busquets who do the groundwork. Every great player stands on the shoulders of his teammates.

It's even the case that mistakes at the back can cause problems at the front, because success in football often hinges on small margins – a positional difference of less than a metre, for example. So if the ball is moving too slowly, your opponent has time to get that bit closer to you. If the ball's moving quickly, there's a chance that he's going to arrive too late. Those are the sort of details I mean. In top-level football they're countless, but they also determine the style of play. Not many coaches have the quality to teach this, and players become more stressed as a result. That often compromises talent. I like technical players who can also think in terms of the team's interests. I've already mentioned Iniesta and Xavi, who disprove entirely the theory that only physically strong footballers with a lot of running ability can play in their positions. A lot of coaches think that way, and choose muscle over technique in midfield. You also see this in the use of the 4-3-3 system. It's made for Dutch football, but a lot of coaches can no longer cope with this attacking style of play. So you see teams playing deeper and deeper, hoping they might get the chance to counter-attack. But anyone with the guts to use 4-3-3 in the right way will be rewarded in the end. As long as the right players are chosen for the system.

These days everything is seen in terms of the solution. Everyone uses videos, analyses and whatever to explain everything. Solve it yourself! That is what I have always said to people. Take a counter-attack, with one defender against two attackers. How do the attackers avoid being offside? Let them work that one out for themselves. Quality also involves seeing what the other person sees. It's the same with solutions. If you're a manager, don't spoon-feed them, let them find the solution for themselves. That applies to the coaches too. I still remember when Barcelona played against Atlético Madrid. José Eulogio Gárate, who wasn't exactly a world-class footballer, was their striker, and whatever we did and however we played, he always got three chances to score. We racked our brains as to how to solve this. We tried to put ourselves in the position of the striker. We talked it over for a while until someone mentioned that he was really good at losing his marker. But of course he could only do that if he was marked. So I said, 'You know what we'll do? We'll stop marking him.' They told me I'd lost my marbles. But that was the solution. Gárate's typical way of playing was to lure a defender towards him, which made it easier for him to shake him off a second later. His way of thinking was just a bit more advanced than ours. So in the next match we left him on his own and stopped running with him. Someone said, 'Yes, but what if he scores two goals?' I said, 'Then we've been unlucky.'

After that we had no more trouble with Gárate. Without an opponent he didn't know what to do. He had lost his bearings, because the man-marker turned out to be his reference point. We'd solved that by thinking differently. Everyone initially panicked, but you've got to try those things out to get to the root of the problem. That's why football is always the foundation as far as I'm concerned, and in principle I'm opposed to all the innovations we're talking about these days. Like goal-line cameras. Football is the only sport played purely with the feet. That's why the chance of mistakes is so much greater. There are no time-outs, which means that coaching during the match is even more difficult. And the likelihood of mistakes is increased yet again.

You see that in the rules of the game as well. They even involve subjective elements such as the awarding of a goal when the ball hasn't crossed the goal line and vice versa. So after the game's over we go to a bar and start talking about it. Things like that create debate and atmosphere. You do some talking and you have a drink. It's all part of the game. Use goal-line technology and the whole discussion has gone. The best thing about discussing football is that every-one can say what they like, and even though someone might be mostly wrong, they're always partly right. Of course it's terrible that in the England–Germany match in the 2010 World Cup a good goal by Frank Lampard wasn't awarded. But rather than talking about cameras you can also debate whether the ref or the linesman were good enough. Isn't the question we should be asking – could they too be coached better?

Football is about both quality and mistakes. Large and small mistakes are constantly being made across the whole pitch. Someone finds himself on his own in front of the goalkeeper but doesn't score; someone else misses a penalty – this is just the way the game works. I can still remember a match in the English FA Cup years ago when the keeper stopped three penalties. What do you do in this instance? Fire the manager? Sack the players who failed to score? Of course not – these things happen, because everyone understands that there are moments of opportunity in every game. Usually they are taken, sometimes they are missed. But is it right to show understanding for a player who misses an open goal, but not for a referee who misjudges a situation? Or do we say, 'They're all on the pitch, let them get on with it, goodbye and goodnight.'

Of course, everyone has to fulfil the same basic criteria. The players on the pitch are trained to the max, so the officials should be trained to the max as well. But because football is a game of errors, the officials will sometimes make them too, just as top scorers miss chances and the best goalkeepers let balls slip through their fingers. These are mistakes that millions of people will talk about for days, months and sometimes even years. That's the great thing about football, and we need to keep on seeing it that way. That's also why it's so important for football to remain under the control of footballers, from the pitch upwards, right to the boardroom. Maybe it's a bit primitive, but that's just how I think and that's why I've clashed with directors so often. They want to decide what happens on the pitch from the boardroom, while I think the people on the pitch should determine what the directors do. Directors always take second place as far as I'm concerned. What I've almost always noticed about them is that they have a top-down attitude. As I mentioned, people who think in this way often feel superior and compelled to convince others that they're right. If instead they think bottom upwards, they come across things that they're not used to, and the roles are switched. Rather than the directors explaining something to you, you have to explain it to them. And that's usually when the problems start. They think you're talking nonsense, because they've never learned it that way themselves.

What directors don't understand is that thinking based on football is the essence of what we do and why people love the game. It's also the basis of coaching people inside a club. In such a system, those at top management level are mostly guiding processes that other people have set in motion. A CEO or chairman shouldn't be the decision-maker. The decision-maker is the one who is responsible for the team – the manager. He decides if someone ought to run harder or sprint further, or doesn't know what he's doing. That's not the job of a director. A director needs to be able to analyse what the club as a commercial entity needs, and find the best solutions for it. That's his job. It's from the pitch that you can sense what the public wants. The customer is king. Don't forget that football, even at the top level, is primarily an entertainment. That's always been my philosophy, and that's never going to change. If you see how empty the stadiums sometimes are in Italy, and how few goals are scored in the English Premier League, you might seriously wonder whether these two great foot-balling nations are on the right path. Two countries where commerce has taken a particular hold.

The potential for such problems is only going to increase in the future, particularly now that China has taken an interest in top-level football. That strikes me as a perfectly natural development, because football has spread over the whole world. And if you want to be a force in the world, you have to be involved in world sport, whether it's the Olympic Games or football. But there always has to be a particular kind of balance. The Chinese might think they can buy and buy and the fans will all come, but if the foundations aren't good, where do you start? You have to be in a position to see the whole. That's why I have followed developments in Japan with great interest. There are lots of parallels with America. In America, twenty years on from the foundation of MLS, they're still waiting to see whether a single footballer can make all the difference and they'll finally join the world's top-ranking teams. Better and better footballers are coming along who can play at higher and higher levels, even in Europe. The same is true of Japan and the J.League.

Of course, it's fabulous that for the last twenty-five years every continent has been enthralled by top-level football. The recent Chinese involvement is the latest phase of a great development, but the most important thing in football's emerging territories, just as in its established ones, is for the game itself to be central in terms of both vision and execution. Only in that way can the newcomers build their own identities and avoid being mere copies of what's there already. An American supporter must be able to recognize himself in his team, just as the Chinese supporter will have to in due course. At Barcelona and Ajax and in the Dutch team I've learned how important it is for people to be able to identify with football. To be part of something special, something that suits them emotionally. Above all, that process must be guided from the field. If that happens in a good and professional way, commerce and club politics will inevitably follow suit.

13

It's probably clear that I'm first and foremost a lover of a magnificent sport. I'm often critical about Dutch football, because I am concerned about how we are dealing with the sport and some of our talents. That's why I'll try to explain as simply as possible how I think football should be played, in a way that the players themselves enjoy but which also speaks to the public, and lies at the heart of the philosophy of Total Football. Everybody knows I like an attacking style of football, but to be able to attack you have to defend by pushing forward, and in order to do that you have to put pressure on the ball. To make this as easy as possible for all the players you have to create as many lines as you can. The man with the ball will then always have someone in front of him and someone next to him. The space between the man with the ball and these two teammates should never be more than ten metres. When there is too much space, it will only increase the risks.

In principle I like to use five lines, excluding the goalkeeper: the back four, a central midfielder playing from the back, two wider midfielders outside him pushing forward, one striker playing from deep or up front and two attackers on the wings. In an attacking formation the field of play is from the bottom half of the centre circle to the opponent's penalty area. This creates a pitch of forty-five metres in length and sixty metres wide, with a gap of about nine metres between the lines.

Why are these distances so important? Because every gap can be covered more easily and more efficiently, and there will always be enough players behind the ball. Note that as soon as Barcelona put on the pressure when they lose the ball, you never see anyone more than ten metres away from a teammate, on top of which everyone's in motion, which means that the attempt to win the ball back is fast and purposeful. This reveals a mistake made by many Dutch clubs, since on too many occasions the central midfielder has to play pushing forward instead of lying deep, and this makes him play too close to the striker. If one of the other midfielders moves inside to close the gap, then the left or right back or the winger will have to defend a space of twenty to thirty metres instead of ten. The players can't link-up, and the team loses control of the game.

Up front you play with one striker and two players on the wings. A deep-lying striker or a striker who pushes up makes no difference when playing with five lines. Marco van Basten and I are generally acknowledged to have been Holland's best players, and while I played as a forward from deep, van Basten was a real striker.

The lines should be close together so an attacker in possession can try something and there will always be six or seven teammates who can cover for him. Furthermore, when you play like this you avoid always passing the ball to a player standing next to you. And then we finally get rid of the false sense of controlling a match which Dutch clubs often suffer from.

When the five lines are used correctly and everybody does what he needs to do, it will create triangles on the pitch, which are essential to your tactics. One player focuses on passing the ball, one on receiving the ball and the third will try to move into space to receive the next pass. In short, people sometimes make football incredibly complicated, but it works best when we just keep it simple. Attacking effectively is mostly a question of the correct application of technique, the use of space, defending towards the front and putting pressure on the ball.

Taking this a step further, I use those five lines as my starting point. It's essential that everybody realizes that the build-up starts when the goalkeeper has the ball. He is the first attacking player and in most of these situations defenders will react quicker than attackers, with one of the full backs already moving forward and available to receive the ball, and by passing the ball to him the first team move is set up. The attacking winger now has to run forward to create the space for the full back. In the meantime, the first line of defenders, in other words the opponent's forwards, has been outplayed and you are setting up an attack. The opponent has to make choices that stop the full back going forward, and the trick is to anticipate this.

I will give two simple examples of when lines need to work together. First, when your striker moves to the right, one of the two opposition central defenders has to follow him and the other one has to move up to cover the extra-man situation that has been created by your full back running forward. In this tactic the left winger and the striker are now facing one-on-one situations. The second possibility is for the left back to pass the ball hard twenty metres forward to the striker, who then passes it back to a forward-moving right midfielder. If the midfielder has timed his run correctly he will have an advantage over his opponent, which creates one-on-one situations on the right-hand side of the pitch.

The idea of these tactics is to surprise the opposition and to create uncertainty. For example, when the left back has passed the ball via a midfielder to his left winger, and he can dribble past his opponent, then anything can happen in front of goal. When he crosses the ball the striker will move from the right side towards the near post, thus creating space for the right midfielder. Johan Neeskens scored plenty of goals using this tactic. In this attacking movement three-quarters of the team are behind the ball and everybody is facing the goal. This takes away the risk of a counter-attack and you are in the right position to pick up the second ball and to defend by pushing forward.

It's important that when the left back has the ball, the goalie and the other defenders are organizing the team. While the attack is set up, the defenders and midfielders are ready to act in case you lose possession. You can take this one step further by having your striker put pressure on their goalkeeper when he has the ball. This increases the tempo and the goalie is forced to play quicker, and if your defenders and midfielders are in the right position you make it extra difficult for your opponent. The striker is now the first defender, while only moments before his goalkeeper was the first attacker. What this shows is that you always have to think ahead, both as an individual and as a team. This way of playing football can be taught fairly easily, and that's why I am surprised when I see that Dutch teams aren't capable of building up moves this way. They pass the ball sideways instead of passing it forward, but this doesn't solve the problem, only moves it to another part of the pitch.

The space on the pitch is the essential factor, especially creating space for yourself, and to do that setting up a move or set-piece is crucial. Often you have to start by doing the opposite of what you want to achieve. For example, when a winger wants the ball to his feet, he will have to run forward and then turn back to receive the ball, just like you sometimes first have to pass the ball back in order to get a long ball forward. Or with corners, when you run towards the ball before the corner is taken in order to draw defenders out of the penalty area.

Players in every position, especially up front, have to cope with these kind of situations, and they affect not only the move itself, but also how the rest of the team anticipate it. Setting a move in motion should never be a stand-alone action – the beauty of football, is that every action, in every position, somehow is linked with other actions elsewhere on the pitch. Take the example above regarding the winger. To receive the ball to feet, he first has to create a situation that will allow him to run forward, but if at the same time his team's striker moves into the same space, the winger can no longer perform his intended action. That is why it annoys me when, in such a situation, people blame the winger when the problem has been caused by the striker. I can't remember how many times I have clashed with reporters who focused on the actions of one person without realizing that his game was being compromised by others. His teammates failed to make use of his abilities. Especially for wingers, the interaction between the set-up and the action itself is crucial. That this is a serious issue nowadays is shown when one side is reduced to ten players. This should cede the advantage, but more and more you can see the team with the extra man getting into trouble since all of a sudden they don't know what to do with the additional space when the opponent pulls back. Often they just knock the ball around in defence rather than applying pressure.

The only way to avoid this is to play one-on-one across the entire pitch. The first advantage this brings is a higher tempo, because all opposing players will be under pressure and when they lose the ball you will immediately have space and outnumber them. At that moment, the whole team should be aware of the space to give your extra player as many chances as possible to make a decisive move. When you play like this, the opponent cannot afford to make mistakes. But you can, because you will have an extra player between your defence and midfield. He has to be positioned there to have a bigger chance of intercepting the ball and to keep the pressure on. Playing like this does not guarantee a win, but it does guarantee that you will create five or six big chances to score.

It's also important to see how you can make a teammate play well and your opponent play badly. So, for example, you can help a teammate by passing the ball to his stronger foot. This might seem simple, even unimportant, but in a good team you don't often see a left-footed player receiving the ball on his right foot. Similarly, when you know that the player you are marking prefers to go round you one way, position yourself such that he is forced to go the other way with the ball on his weaker foot. This might all seem elementary, but unfortunately even at the highest level you see players – and even coaches – hardly thinking about things such as this. Everyone is keen to talk about style of play and tactics, but in most cases these are used in the wrong way. Take formations. For me it isn't about 4-3-3 or

4-4-2 or 5-3-2, but an adaptation to the style of play in which you take the edge off your opponent, and turn his strength into his weakness.

The art of making your opponent play badly mostly has to do with the kind of players you put on the pitch. English teams usually defend one-on-one at the back, and the central defenders excel in the air, so against them you field a roaming striker who takes short passes. You also put two deep-lying wingers in the team because the English aren't used to that either. You have to put on pressure towards the front, which means that the English players never get to do the calm build-up they're used to. In cases like that something else comes to the surface: the difference between someone with good or bad technique is agility. Applying pressure quickly means that agility has to come to the fore, and most English defenders have a problem with that because in the Premier League, when their team wins the ball, they're used to their opponent running not forward but back.

Which brings me to the extra quality of Barcelona. It's not just the presence of someone like Messi that scares opponents, but also the way the team play when they don't have the ball. As soon as they lose possession, everything and everyone is immediately focused on trying to regain the ball. Since they play so close to the opponent's goal their formation remains tight, and when they do get the ball back they pose an immediate threat.

That type of forward play was once also the trademark of Dutch football. Unfortunately, we've moved away from that house style, which is a shame, particularly because Barcelona and Bayern Munich continue to show us how well it works. Also, it's easy to do. Primarily, it requires only that, as a team, you know what to do when you lose the ball. It has little to do with technique or having a player like Messi in the side. It's about the attitude drilled into players from a young age, and that Barcelona do it so effectively has a lot to do with their youth training. It was like that when I was coach there, and it's still the case. Consider the wisdom of putting Ronald Koeman and Pep Guardiola, two attack-minded players with good scoring ability, at the centre of defence. Neither of them was a real defender, and yet it worked because defending is a matter of positioning, agility and ability to attack. If you have those three elements in your team, you don't even need to defend.

In football you always have to be in search of pin-pricks that throw your opponent off course. For example, thinking unconventionally, which takes your opponent out of his comfort zone, just as playing straightforwardly can often produce beautiful football. As we've seen, one good example is switching gear when you lose the ball, particularly if you're an attacking team that's weaker in defence. In a team like that, if you can get your attackers to press high up the pitch, so testing the opposing defenders' agility, which increases their chance of making a bad pass. Here, the attackers are acting as the first defenders, and defending in such a situation means bridging distances of only four to five metres. There are numerous other examples of how problems can be reduced – not by complicated tactical interventions but merely by thinking logically.

In this regard, I have noticed over the last few years that players in attack-minded teams are often poor headers of the ball. In my day the outside right Sjaak Swart scored an unusually high number of goals for a winger, because he could head the ball over his right shoulder. This is a necessary skill when the left winger crosses the ball and the forward moves to the near post and the right winger comes in at the far post. This is why in these situations you often see forwards missing simple chances, because they try to produce a header to their 'good' side, instead of glancing it to the other side – a right winger heading the ball towards goal over his right shoulder. The same goes for defenders, who often score own goals in these situations.

As a footballer you always have to look for things that can hurt your opponent, but they're doing the same thing. As soon as you know that your opponent is trying to take advantage of your weak spot, you have to be able to make a counter move. Just as in the situations I discussed above, the examples I mention here are about reducing problems. In Holland we have let this way of thinking slip away as well, so have fallen behind the rest of Europe. By making it more and more complicated we have lost track of the basics. The most important thing for a player is that he knows how to do the simple actions. I mean passing, receiving, controlling the ball with his chest, being able to use his weaker foot and heading. In short, the basic techniques. These are all skills that anyone can be trained in.

Learning to pass the ball correctly is simply a matter of repeating it over and over. This might be boring, but you are honing the most essential aspect of the game. The same goes for receiving the ball – it is tedious to do, but you make quick progress. Then you have to combine these basic techniques with positional play. That's why I've introduced six-a-side tournaments on the Cruyff Courts, which measure forty-two metres by twenty-eight. In some contexts, I don't mind whether it's four against four, seven versus seven or fifteen against fifteen. As long as it gets people, and especially children, to play football, it's all good. However, as soon as we are truly 'developing' talent, then only six against six will work because boys and girls will then learn the ground rules of 'real' football without realizing it.

First, there are a goalkeeper and five outfield players, meaning you can play with three lines. These lines are so compact that you need to pass the ball correctly to allow a teammate to make a move. There is no *libero*, because everyone is forced to play one-on-one, in attack and in defence. In this situation a player will automatically learn to keep an eye on his opponent and to cover for his teammate. Without telling him to do so, he is already learning positional play. This also applies to the goalkeeper – he not only has to stop the ball, but he also has to cover and sometimes has to contribute to open play. For street football tournaments this is perfect for kids twelve years or younger, and after that age you can always use it as a training exercise. Simply put, it forces you to play in small spaces, one-on-one, and use simple technique. You can forget about easily playing the ball around in defence. Just passing the ball to the player next to you teaches you to avoid making the mistakes that many Dutch players currently make.

I'm mostly trying to explain how important it is that new talent should work on the ground rules from a young age. The sooner they master those, the more they learn later on, and, to be honest, there isn't much point moving on if you haven't sorted out the foundations. Only then can you start talking about putting the ideal team together, formed with players who aren't just unusually talented, but who have all mastered the basics of football.

*

I wouldn't usually bother even trying to name a team from the best footballers ever, simply because in most cases there's hardly any difference in quality. Nearly all former and current footballers at the top of the game fulfil the conditions required to make it into the highest rank. They're also, without exception, gifted, which means that they have no trouble reaching the highest possible level in another position. I think that Marco van Basten could have been a player of international class as a right back. Still, it's something I'm often asked, so . . .

By now it's probably clear what type of players that I look for. Players with outstanding technique, a lot of insight and usually a high degree of specialization. That last quality in particular ensures the extra gift that marks out top footballers. You also have to use it, rather than subordinating a talent like that to the collective. I'll turn that round. The collective interest is served if a talented player like that is used to the best effect, and the trick at the top is to use all the talent you've got to the best advantage and at the same time to form a good team. If that works, your squad escapes grey mediocrity because of the added value it contains. For the ideal squad I also try and find a formula in which talent is used to the maximum in every case. The qualities of one player have to complement the qualities of another. So behind wingers like Piet Keizer (left) and the Brazilian Garrincha (right), I'd put midfielders like Bobby Charlton (left) and Alfredo Di Stéfano (right). Both top footballers who aren't just technically and tactically brilliant, but who also fit together well physically. That puts them in an excellent position to do extra work for stylists like Keizer and Garrincha, rather than the other way round. Full backs like Ruud Krol (left) and Carlos Alberto (right) also contribute their insight, technique and speed as support for Charlton and Di Stéfano, to keep those two midfielders from getting overrun.

When drawing up this fantasy squad I've also thought of characters like Franz Beckenbauer, Pep Guardiola, Diego Maradona and Pelé. Pelé and Maradona in particular are a perfect match, because Pelé's enormous sense of responsibility connects nicely with Maradona's individualism. I know for sure that during the match Pelé would watch over Diego as a kind of guide, because footballers have a perfect sense for that kind of thing, and Maradona would give something back to Pelé, which would allow him to be fully appreciated. In my ideal squad I'd choose the legendary Lev Yashin as goalkeeper since, with this impressive collection of talent, it can hardly do any harm to have a reassuring father figure to bring all those stars down to earth.

In all discussions about football I deliberately avoid the term 'willing runner' or talking about a player's stamina, especially since over the past few years it's got completely out of control. It's started a process whereby the footballer has to run more and gets to spend less time playing football, while the trick is to use the space on the pitch in such a way that it's the ball and not the feet that do the work. This brings us to the natural transition from the individual analysis of each player to collective performance. Technique, insight and above all talent are all present within each individual, and the eleven individuals together have to use the space on the pitch to work well as a whole. Next you need insight – the ability to judge who should position themselves where, in such a way that the team stays together. I still get very annoyed when I see lines that are far apart, which means that one part of the team is forced to cover enormous distances. Of course, the trick is to keep the players close together. Only then do you create a situation whereby the ball can do the work. Then success automatically depends on technique, which is necessary to use the ball and the space well, and that's why, in theory, it's the simplest thing in the world. You need insight to keep the lines close together, and technique to let the ball do the work efficiently and last of all you need the talent to do the job – it's not about running, it's just about keeping your eyes open and playing. If you can master that then you have mastered the essence of Total Football.

14

People used to tell me all the time that I was stupid because I never completed my education, but life has taught me far more than any book. And, ultimately, experience of life is knowledge. The Cruyff Foundation is one of the things that developed from everything that I've seen and done, and the people I've met. The foundation works with schools, sports federations, governments, businesses and other partners, and simply put its goal is to give every young person the chance to play sport and exercise every day, whatever their background or abilities.

I'm very proud of its success, and I even think I have gained from it more than I have given. Someone in a wheelchair is often seen as somehow less valid. Unsurprisingly, the person in the wheelchair has a different view: he or she just gets on with it. Thanks to those the foundation has helped, I never think I'm too old for anything, or that there's anything I can't do. It's also great to see what the project has unleashed in colleagues, volunteers, ambassadors, parents and even whole families – they've all dedicated themselves to making something happen. My role is mostly to be there to receive the bouquets and the compliments, because most of the work is no longer in my hands, which is just how it should be.

The idea started with Eunice Kennedy Shriver's request for me to become ambassador to the Special Olympics in

America when I was living there. Her organization also had a branch in Barcelona, where the wife of the president of Catalonia was involved, so I stayed in touch later on too, when I was back in Spain. There were lots of things I couldn't do at that point, because being coach of Barcelona didn't leave me with much time, but that changed when I was no longer active in football day-to-day. More and more often I was asked to contribute to all kinds of charities. Sometimes it went well, sometimes it didn't, so I learned through bitter experience, and was able to talk to people about what I'd come up against. I realized that eventually, whatever you do, and at whatever level, you need some help. That produced the idea of doing something from within an organization of my own, based on my own experiences. When my father-in-law discovered that I was becoming interested in that sort of area, he brought things together.

In 1997 Cor Coster put me in contact with the child relief agency Terre des Hommes. Workers from that organization first helped me set up the Johan Cruyff Welfare Foundation, although we later decided to keep the name simple – just the Cruyff Foundation. When the time was right to appoint a professional director, Carole Thate appeared on the scene. She was the captain of the Dutch hockey team, and she contacted us because she'd read something about my new ambitions, and she was extremely interested. After that I let everything take its course, as I've often done in my life, because I've always been curious by nature and prefer just to let things happen. Terre des Hommes set the organization up, and the Postcode Lottery made a very generous financial contribution, so we were able to open our own office at the Olympic Stadium and later in Barcelona, and before I was aware of it I was busy doing something new which has enriched me in many respects. First of all, as I've already alluded to, I've always been attracted by the spiritual buoyancy that a lot of disabled people show. Often they first have to take a step back before they can start to do anything. Sport and games are two things that can boost the spirit in a relaxed way for the other battles they have to fight.

In the early days of the foundation I went to India, and that packed a punch. I saw close up how millions of children were literally living in the street, which was an extraordinary sight to behold. Because I'm the way I am, my immediate thought was, 'What are we going to do here?' Because we had to do something. But the immediate reaction I had was that there was a gigantic problem which was completely insoluble. That sort of thought process sends you back to where you started, and you realize you have to learn to set personal boundaries by asking yourself who you are, what you can do and how you can do it.

In the context of a challenge like this, I ended up surrounded by people who didn't see me as a famous person, who instead wanted to see what my qualities were, and what I was going to do to make a difference. They set things in motion, and just by trying to help I discovered what my own shortcomings were. It was a liberating feeling to be put on the spot like that, to have to prove myself all over again to a group of strangers, and for the first time I could ever remember people were not turning to me as a leader only because of my reputation. After about six months I realized that the structure of the foundation needed to be improved, but I didn't really have a say over what happened next, especially when I found myself at odds with my own organization. What we did agree on was that we had to gain tighter control of the project, become more self-sufficient so that we wouldn't have to contract so many things out, and that's how the idea of the Cruyff Institute and schools came about. We were dealing with disabled people, with disadvantaged young members of society, and we were using sport and games to do it. In that context practical experience is much more important than academic know-how. When it turned out that that kind of practical training didn't exist, we decided to set it up ourselves. That's when you start searching for a model to base your idea on, and I looked in the mirror and came to the conclusion that I should be the model for this. I have a whole lot of understanding about what I've always done. Not from academic study, but from practical experience.

Then I took a look at whether among the existing forms of business training there was one that suited me. There wasn't, and it became very clear that many of the sports business management training courses at universities were taught from the perspective of looking down at the pitch from the boardroom, which was exactly what I didn't want. I just wanted the lessons to reach the young people who were looking up to the boardroom from the pitch. They had to know the same things to be successful in the boardroom, but, as it should be in football, the insight had to come completely from the other side, which meant thinking from the pitch up. To address this situation, we decided to establish the Cruyff Institute to educate athletes, sports and business people in sports management. We began in Amsterdam in 1999, and now we have campuses in Barcelona, Mexico, Sweden and Peru and our online courses are available in more and more countries around the world.

If it was Terre des Hommes that helped me set up the Cruyff Foundation, the Cruyff Institute was, thanks to my son-in-law Todd Beane, founded entirely according to my own ideas. For that Todd deserves a great deal of credit, because particularly at the beginning there seemed to be major disputes about everything and with everyone. Fights with all kinds of education authorities and all kinds of ministries. On the academic side of things everything had to be shaken-up as well. The players couldn't come to the school, which meant that the school had to come to them, which solved one of the big problems that athletes looking to educate themselves face. Take the 2014 Winter Olympics, which were held in Sochi in January. The institute's exams would normally be held in November, but we stipulated that they first had to go and compete and then they could come back in February to do their exams, or, as I told some of the students: 'After the games we'll put you through the mill, but first go and get those medals.' All of which meant that for the Cruyff Institute, performance in sport takes precedence over exam timetables, because it is based on the philosophy that this is the way in which you get the maximum out of the athlete. He or she knows that afterwards they must devote themselves to their studies completely, and the proof of the pudding was in the eating, since the Cruyff Institute for Sport Studies has an incredibly high success rate in delivering both medals and excellent exam results.

You see the same thing in the coaching masterclasses we hold. One of the most important aspects of the programme is that the coach gets to know him or herself very well first, so it isn't just a matter of what the lecturers know about their subjects, it's what they know about themselves, what they themselves can do and what they are capable of. You can't analyse someone else until you can analyse yourself, otherwise you always use your own standards to analyse other people when in fact you should be using theirs. You have to reach the stage whereby you can step outside yourself in order to judge someone else, rather than basing judgement on your own experiences. That doesn't help a student: it's your baggage, not theirs. The athlete is paramount, but problems emerge when teachers look at things from a completely different perspective.

As coaches, it is our job to tailor the coaching process to benefit the athlete, and that's often confrontational. This isn't a criticism of the general teaching profession, but they're often hamstrung by the fact that they have to follow a curriculum that's been decreed from above. For us, on the other hand, it's a kind of adventure where we reverse this. When we put together our programme we ask the athlete what they want to know, which aspect we should be addressing in our teaching. It's striking that a lot of our teachers feel great about this style of learning. To shape the Masters in Sport Management and coaching courses as we have done was certainly essential – but we now need to revolutionize the entire approach to sports coaching across the board. And it is working – bit by bit, people in sport are starting to think from the pitch towards the boardroom rather than the other way round. I'm convinced that the more things go in that direction, the better the sport can be managed, and the better results we will achieve.

The Cruyff Institute is still growing, but so, importantly, are its online training sessions, spreading throughout the world and reaching thousands of students and associations at leading universities as well as at many clubs and federations. In the Netherlands it has continued to grow, first with Cruyff Universities providing graduate level courses, and later Cruyff Colleges, which provide vocational training, and when I look back, it's brilliant to reflect that the schools came into being because of problems within the foundation that we solved by deciding to train people ourselves. That's why it feels really good that my daughter Susila has been on the board of the Cruyff Foundation for years, because she is someone who thinks and feels the way I do. That puts me at ease about the future, because it's really become my thing, which will go on long after I'm no longer around.

The foundation is now run in the Netherlands by Niels Meijer, a basketball international whom we've fast-tracked via Cruyff University to succeed Carole Thate. Carole had come so far by now that I thought the time was ripe for her to take over all my management, which is another example of us solving our own problem from within. Carole has now brought all my activities within the umbrella organization the World of Johan Cruyff, which includes not only the foundation and schools but also Cruyff Classics, Cruyff Football and Cruyff Library. Something that started almost twenty years ago as a fringe project with disabled children has now grown into an organization with an incredible number of activities.

The Cruyff Courts are another idea that developed out of all kinds of experiences. It started with the six-a-sides, then came Aron Winter's farewell Winter Ball with a football match on artificial turf in the Concertgebouw, after which the pitch was donated to Winter's home town, Lelystad. The response to this gesture was enormous and we realized that the old playing fields which used to be found in so many neighbourhoods and districts had been swallowed up by development. So we decided to do something about it. What started in 2003 in one of the finest concert halls in the Netherlands had by 2016 grown to 208 mini-pitches distributed all over the world. An unexpected bonus is that a lot of the courts have been sponsored by footballers. That's why I think it's so special that the winner of the annual Johan Cruyff Prize for the Dutch Player of the Year can choose the location of a Cruyff Court to be named after him. In that way I'm trying to give the most talented players, who act as role models even at a young age, a different kind of responsibility.

Lately we'd been running into problems finding suitable sites for Cruyff Courts, particularly in the Netherlands, where, because it is a small country, there isn't that much unused space. Then it finally dawned on us that there's one place where young people have to go every day, and that's school. We went and had a look at several schools we thought might benefit and found that the area of the school most neglected by students was often the sports pitch. So we talked to the kids and the school staff and tried to find ways to make the pitches more attractive. That's how we ended up starting 'Playground 14', the idea being to develop a spot near the school where kids can play and do sport whenever they like. By now we can barely keep up with the applications as so many schools want to get involved, but somehow we're going to solve that one too, because this just has to happen.

Some schools have even taken things a step further, using the project as a springboard to organize all kinds of competitions as well as tournaments against other schools. Getting children more active doesn't just reduce the likelihood of diabetes or obesity, it also helps to solve the childcare problem for working parents. Parents can drop their children off before school has started and they can play sport for half an hour before lessons begin, so everyone wins. This is another example of how logical thinking can produce simple solutions to complex and longstanding problems. This is just how it works in sport. I've said often that playing simple football is the most complicated thing there is, but if you have the basic qualities – the fundamental skills – you can always perform better in the end. That's why the world of sport is the most beautiful world there is. The only problem is that these days football is in the hands of people who have never played the game, and the problems have gotten so bad that it is almost as though we are waiting for it all to collapse, so we can start again.

The experiences I have been through in sport have given me a vast store of knowledge that needs to be shared, and everything I have learned has been poured into the Cruyff Foundation, so that others can profit from my experiences. Allowing children to have access to these kinds of open sporting facilities is common in America, as opposed to Europe where, traditionally, if children want to play sport they have to do it through a club. That's why I have a huge amount of respect for Guus Hiddink, who was able to bring together all the strands of what we taught in a shortened coaching course for former internationals at the KNVB when he was the Dutch national coach. Rather than making them study for four years, he appointed Frank Rijkaard and Ronald Koeman as his assistants, and made them follow the course as well. After the 1998 World Cup, when the Dutch team reached the semi-final, they received their diplomas. This approach circumvented the whole laborious administrative process and just let these brilliant players get on and do what they do best, which is to teach players how to play football. Phillip Cocu and Frank de Boer were later also able to profit from the same programme. People like Guus are vital if we are to change the classical thought patterns within the sport. They are the ones who never lose sight of the play on the field, even when they're sitting in the boardroom.

This philosophy doesn't apply only to football: during the 2012 Olympic Games I watched Sebastian Coe with admiration. It was fascinating to see someone teaching people to think from the athletics track upwards to the boardroom. Coe has a keen sense of what he knows, what his abilities are, and at the same time understands which areas need to be improved. Having watching what Coe did in London, it was an enormous honour to be invited by him to the Paralympic Games. It was an unforgettable experience and we were able to use training courses to give a number of disabled athletes involved with the Cruyff Foundation some experience for the 2016 games in Rio. We often complain in sport about a crisis, but in London I saw athletes in action who, in spite of all the problems they have, gave it their all, and tried at the same time to keep on getting better. These Paralympians are my role models. They showed how you join hands to improve situations. You can't do anything on your own, you have to work together, and that's the connection I'd like to see between all the activities I'm involved with, just as happened with Cruyff Courts and the Playground 14 project. Governments could contribute too, by placing greater emphasis on gym and sports lessons in schools. I'd go a step further:

sports should be compulsory. This would benefit everyone as it would save the state a fortune if people lived healthier lives. Diabetes is threatening to become an epidemic because young people move around much less. Children don't just spend hours every day sitting down at school and over their homework; these days they also spend hours sitting at their computers and watching TV instead of running around outdoors. We all need to put our shoulders to the wheel and guide them, not just by making it clear that what they're doing is bad for them, but at the same time offering solutions.

In that respect I'm probably an idealist, whether it has to do with football, the foundation or schools, I always try to do things in a positive way, and above all make it clear that nothing is impossible. It's something I got from my RE lessons at school. I'm a believer, but I don't have a religion. For me it has more to do with a way of thinking and behaving, not about adhering to the details of a particular faith. Ultimately, it's a matter of philosophy. The Christian faith has the ten commandments to live by; I myself have fourteen rules which I would class as fundamental wisdoms. How do you treat people, what do you do to help them? Where that's concerned, some sort of creed is important as a way of giving you a set of bearings, without going to extremes. Being influenced by people who have sorted things out. Thinking how something can be achieved. How it can be made better. What extras you can add.

I read an article once about the building of the pyramids in Egypt. It turns out that some of the numbers coincide completely with natural laws – the position of the moon at certain times and so on. And it makes you think: how is it possible that those ancient people built something so scientifically complex? They must have had something that we don't, even though we always think that we're a lot more advanced than they were. Take Rembrandt and van Gogh: who can match them today? When I think that way, I'm increasingly convinced that everything is actually possible. If they managed to do the impossible nearly five thousand years ago, why can't we do it today? That applies equally to football, but also to something like the Cruyff Courts and school sports grounds.

My fourteen rules are set out for every court and every school sports ground to follow. They are there to teach young people that sports and games can also be translated into everyday life. To see them working you don't need higher mathematics, because it happens whenever you collaborate with a colleague. Thinking, with a glass of wine in your hand: it's not done yet, there's still something missing. Working with sport like that always gives me a fantastic feeling.

The Fourteen Rules of Johan Cruyff

1. Team Player – 'To accomplish things, you have to do them together'

2. Responsibility – 'Take care of things as if they were your own'

3. Respect – 'Respect one another'

4. Integration – 'Involve others in your activities'

5. Initiative – 'Dare to try something new'

6. Coaching – 'Always help each other within a team'

7. Personality – 'Be yourself'

8. Social Involvement – 'Interaction is crucial, both in sport and in life'

9. Technique – 'Know the basics'

10. Tactics – 'Know what to do'

11. Development – 'Sport strengthens body and soul'

12. Learning – 'Try to learn something new every day'

13. Play Together – 'An essential part of any game'

14. Creativity – 'Bring beauty to the sport'

The conflicts I have experienced with Ajax and Barcelona have taught me how life sometimes takes strange and unexpected turns. That's why I take it as it is, and my family plays a central part. In spite of moving house so often we've remained a really tight family, and that's what's kept me sane during the most difficult times. I'm grateful for the constant support I've had, most of all from my wife, Danny, and the fact that in the Netherlands, Spain and America I always had a clear view of everything I was doing. Danny, the three kids, the three dogs and the cat. Wherever I ended up living, the fact we were all together always gave me the feeling of really being at home. So, there's no point asking what would have happened if I hadn't left Ajax in 1987. When I look at my Spanish-born grandchildren and see how happy my children are in Barcelona, it's all the clearer to me that this is how it had to be.

But I still miss the Netherlands. I remain proud of my country, with all its advantages and disadvantages. It might be small, but it's full to the brim with quality. You won't find so many multinationals per square metre anywhere else in the world. Even New York used to belong to us before we sold it. On the other hand, we're not always the nicest people and I'm a product of that, because if you need someone to moan about something then I'm your man! But above all the Dutch are a unique people, and I'll always keep telling that to my children and grandchildren.

Because of the life I've lived it's clear that Chantal, Susila and Jordi don't have a normal childhood behind them. And my fame has put pressure on our family too. Whenever I played a good match I was the king, both on the terraces and in the school playground too, but if I performed badly, my kids suffered the fallout. I've always ensured that, whether I was playing well or badly, I didn't change as a father; I was always the same dad. This is why I am so grateful to Danny, who had a pretty spartan upbringing herself. She ensured that our children were given the right standards and values. At Christmas we saw to it that our kids bought presents for children worse off than themselves, and every year after they'd wrapped the family gifts to put under the tree, they delivered their parcels to various children's homes. Danny was the brains behind that initiative and others, and it was the kind of thing that helped keep the kids' feet firmly on the ground. We also taught our son and daughters to always follow their own emotions, because it's important to take your own advice, particularly to make well-considered decisions. And yes, even then it's win or lose; sometimes you get brickbats and sometimes bouquets, but you've got to learn to deal with both.

Having finished his footballing career, my son Jordi is now getting on with the next phase of his life. I find it amusing that he's opinionated too, and that he makes his own mistakes. We're open with each other, we discuss everything, but he always has to take the important decisions himself. It is Danny, though, who has provided the balance for me, which I have always needed and have always been grateful for. She compensates for all the things that I can't see, but which are important in my situation, in my immediate circle. So when I come home there's a flower in a vase. Even if I didn't buy it myself, it's great to see it and smell it when I open the door. I think that kind of grounding is crucial. A balance that never tips off to one side or the other.

Where the kids are concerned, we always left their choice of sport up to them. One played football, another rode horses. My oldest daughter, Chantal, probably has the widest range of abilities, but I think she's the least athletic of the three. When she had to do cross-country running or swimming or whatever she was one of the best, but as soon as anyone mentioned training she didn't want to know. Susila, on the other hand, is a lot more disciplined, and she's reached a high standard in showjumping. In the past she has cleared one metre forty-five, and that's really very high. She started riding when we came back to Amsterdam from America and she took it further after we moved to Barcelona, and came very close to getting on the Spanish Olympic team. She even trained with the top English equestrian Michael Whitaker, from whom she still hears now and again. But when she was about to take the last step she had problems with the muscles that support her kneecaps. It was very sad and annoying, but Susila is still wild about horses. Chantal's son has taken over from her to some extent, and he's now jumping one metre forty.

In terms of football, to some extent I've passed the

baton to Jordi. I don't know if Jordi's going to do the same to one of my grandchildren, but they have the necessary character and are technically outstanding. So who knows? They still have a long way to go. A very long way.

My children have grown into strong personalities. They work hard, they speak foreign languages – Chantal has seven – and they've made their own lives. Even though we have a strong bond as a family, we give each other room. Everyone is constantly travelling all over the world, doing their own thing. But wherever we are, we all stay in contact. Always. At the moment I've got eight grandchildren. Six boys and two adopted girls. I feel blessed to have been able to get to know them all, which has been a fantastic experience every bit as good as fatherhood, and it really feels like they are my children, even though we are another generation apart. When I stand back and look at them I see a whole life in progress and it makes me very happy, and I know that it's all been worth the trouble. If I was asked to name the best thing that's ever happened to me, I'd answer my wife, my children and my grandchildren. Thanks to them I feel rich. Very rich.

I've led a full life and can look back on it the way you're supposed to. Indeed, it's been so incredibly intense that I feel like I've lived for a hundred years. I've lived it with authenticity; I've taken things as they've come since I was a boy, including beautiful moments and setbacks, which I've learned are not always caused by mistakes. A setback is probably a sign that you need to make some adjustments. If you learn to think that way, all experiences are translated into something positive. It enriches you as a person. And you learn to be disappointed, but never sad. Luckily, I've overcome all the setbacks. That didn't happen by chance either. I'm an attacker, I'm not scared of anyone, and I'm used to creating things. That's why I've never felt shame. Not even when I lost millions on that pig farm, because I saw very quickly how stupid I'd been. After all, why should somebody who's so good at football and knows so much about it suddenly be an expert on pigs? If you dare to look at yourself in the mirror there's no room for shame, as long as you draw the right lesson from the situation, and as long as you can use your mistakes to continue further along your path. Then it becomes a question of taking your revenge, and luckily I've always been very good at that.

I've had a lot of good luck with the people who've crossed my path. It sounds unbelievable, but because of my crazy life no one is inaccessible to me. One of the first people I met was the engineer Frits Philips, the chairman of the electronics company that bears his name. Anton Drees-mann was another guy I could ring up at any time. As was Horst Dassler from Adidas. I met him, we had a chat and he explained things I had no idea about. Ex-minister Pieter Winsemius is another. I always get on with him as he doesn't talk to me from the perspective of his position, but on the basis of his knowhow. Leen Hollander, one of the advisors at the foundation, has the same quality. And so does the former chairman of the IOC, Juan Antonio Sama-ranch, who used to live in Barcelona. These are all people who are capable of improvising, and who, more import-antly, have no ego. They're also the best in their specialist areas.

This is a big contrast with all the supposedly important people I have encountered, and I'm always struck by how big their egos really are. That's the big difference between people who think simply and speak their mind and people who think they have to stick to a pattern of expectations. I've often experienced that myself. There's no one in football who knows more about tactics, technique and youth training than I do, so why are you debating with me? It's utterly pointless and you'll only do it wrong, so listen to me, benefit from it. How big must your ego be if you can't see that? Luckily, I've listened to the special people around me, who sent me in the right direction in the end.

I'm also someone who remains true to the people close to my heart. Everyone who knows me is aware that friendship is very important to me. I've known my best friend, Rolf Grooteboer, since I was five years old, and when we're together I'm Jopie and he's Dooie. I was always called Jopie when we were kids, and he was Dooie – 'dead boy' – because he never said anything. We know exactly what we get from each other. Because so many different kinds of people have meant something to me, I'm glad I can still talk to young people. Apparently I've kept pace with the times pretty well, I'm sure thanks in large part to all the new technological developments I've been able to take advantage of.

Nothing is ever truly the finished article, and that's why it's so important to think creatively, to keep progressing. Of course, that doesn't mean that all ideas are good, but yours could be the germ of one that inspires other people to go on to perfect it. But if you leave it in the box, nothing is ever going to happen. Absolutely nothing. If you're obliged always to think the way they think at the top, then nothing changes. In my view, nothing has ever been invented by one person. I think that when the light bulb was being created Thomas Edison took charge within a group of very capable people. It's like doing a calculation, when individual figures are combined to deliver a single result. It starts with all kinds of small inputs; it's never complete straight away.

Total Football is just the same. First there were the players, each with their own specific qualities, who were brought together to form a whole. The important trick is to see that potential harmony and use it.

These days that's the biggest failing of people in important positions, both in the sport and outside it. They don't see what they need to see, because they see only themselves. If you are working with people like that, then you might be in charge, but your power is very limited. I know what I'm talking about, because I've been lucky enough to have grown up in a time of innovation. The Beatles, long hair, a revolt against conformity, flower power, take your pick. Such an incredible amount of what has happened over the last fifty years has its roots in that time. Through music, but also through sport. Just think what the Beatles set in motion, both musically and in society. And none of it had anything to do with academic study.

Now things are tipping over again. Creativity is under attack because machines are doing more and more of our thinking for us. Take football. A lot of top-level players have thousands of followers on social media. That's lovely, that's special. If someone has that many followers, it's because people are interested in him and maybe want to learn from him. That's why they follow him. Meanwhile the person with all those followers has to go on learning, but who do the followed follow? Or are they just busy being followed, like people nowadays are famous for being famous? In the end, that popularity becomes just another limitation to what can be done in life. That's why people like Cor Coster, Horst Dassler, Pieter Winsemius and all the others have been so important to me. They didn't just help me avoid mistakes, they also helped me think differently. Which meant that I could go on developing my active footballing career in a way that has given me at least as much satisfaction as being a footballer and a coach.

I was once asked how I would like to be remembered in a hundred years' time. Luckily I don't have to worry about it too much, because I won't be here. But if I had to give an answer I'd say something like, 'As a responsible sportsman.' If I'm to be judged purely as a footballer, then my life would be defined by a period of between fifteen and twenty years, and quite honestly I think that's too limited. My footballing talent was given to me by God. I didn't have to do anything to earn it. It just meant that I got to play a bit of football, and do exactly what I wanted to do. While others said they were off to work, I just went off to play football. So I've been lucky that way. That's why the other things I've done in my life carry more weight with me. I haven't always been understood. As a footballer, as a coach, and also for what I did after all that. But OK, Rembrandt and van Gogh weren't understood either. That's what you learn: people go on bothering you until you're a genius.

Afterword

From Johan Cruyff's Memorial Service at Camp Nou

On Thursday, 24 March 2016, my father passed away, surrounded by his family. His wish was to keep this very private, so his cremation has taken place with only a very small family circle present. Johan clearly stated that he wanted to keep things sober, and above all intimate.

But the family realizes that Johan doesn't belong to us alone, he belongs to everyone. So we are very grateful to FC Barcelona for having stood by us and for holding this memorial here in the stadium. It means that today we can publicly thank the doctor, the hospital and all the people who have looked after my father so well during the last few months of his life.

We are now learning just how good a decision it was to share the loss of Johan with everyone. The love and respect that have been shown are very special. We thank you for the energy that you have given to the family.

We are also proud and happy that everyone has agreed to respect our privacy. We understand that this can sometimes be difficult with a famous father. Where that is concerned, we would again like to thank Barcelona. Everything has always been done in consultation with the family, and our wishes have always been taken into consideration.

So it is particularly lovely that Johan's last signature was to ratify the collaboration between the club and his foundation.

I cannot stress enough how proud my father was of this. He loved Ajax, Barcelona and the Dutch national team, but the foundation was his special child, into which he put all his energy and attention during his final years. That's why we as a family will do everything we can to honour his values and wishes, and to carry them out every day.

Johan belonged to everyone and was a source of inspiration to many. That is also how he should be remembered.

Jordi Cruyff
Tuesday, 29 March 2016

Picture Ackowledgements

Page 1 top and page 2 courtesy of Cruyff Management
Page 1 bottom, page 4, page 7, page 13 top, page 14, page 15 top
    © VI Images via Getty Images
Page 3, page 9 and page 12 bottom © Hollandse Hoogte/REX/
    Shutterstock
Page 5 top © AGIP/Bridgeman Images
Page 5 bottom © Peter Robinson/EMPICS Sport
Page 6 top © AP/Press Association Images
Page 6 bottom © Allsport UK/Allsport
Page 8 top © Bettmann/Getty Images
Page 8 bottom © Bob Thomas/Getty Images
Page 10 © EFE/PA Images
Page 11 © Colorsport/REX/Shutterstock
Page 12 top © *De Telegraaf*/Jan Stappenbeld
Page 13 bottom © Giuliano Bevilacqua/REX/Shutterstock
Page 15 bottom © Koen van Weel/AFP/Getty Images
Page 16 top © Olaf Kraak/AFP/Getty Images
Page 16 bottom © Julian Finney/Getty Images

Estrella Damm
NIKE.COM/FCB
NIKE.COM/FCB
NIKE.COM/FCB
Estrella Damm
QATAR AIRWAYS
QATAR AIRWAYS